Cameras at War

Photo Gear that Captured 100 Years of Conflict: From Crimea to Korea

John Wade

Pen & Sword
MILITARY

First published in Great Britain in 2020 by
Pen & Sword Military
An imprint of
Pen & Sword Books Ltd
Yorkshire – Philadelphia

Copyright © John Wade 2020

ISBN 978 1 52676 010 4

The right of John Wade to be identified as Author of this work has been
asserted by him in accordance with the Copyright, Designs and Patents
Act 1988.

A CIP catalogue record for this book is
available from the British Library.

Typeset by Mac Style
Printed and bound in the UK by
CPI Group (UK) Ltd, Croydon, CR0 4YY

Pen & Sword Books Limited incorporates the imprints of Atlas,
Archaeology, Aviation, Discovery, Family History, Fiction, History,
Maritime, Military, Military Classics, Politics, Select, Transport,
True Crime, Air World, Frontline Publishing, Leo Cooper, Remember
When, Seaforth Publishing, The Praetorian Press, Wharncliffe
Local History, Wharncliffe Transport, Wharncliffe True Crime
and White Owl.

For a complete list of Pen & Sword titles please contact

PEN & SWORD BOOKS LIMITED
47 Church Street, Barnsley, South Yorkshire, S70 2AS, England
E-mail: enquiries@pen-and-sword.co.uk
Website: www.pen-and-sword.co.uk

Or

PEN AND SWORD BOOKS
1950 Lawrence Rd, Havertown, PA 19083, USA
E-mail: Uspen-and-sword@casematepublishers.com
Website: www.penandswordbooks.com

Contents

Introduction   vi

Chapter 1   The Early Years   1

Chapter 2   The Crimean War   7

Chapter 3   Cameras and Photography in 1914   15

Chapter 4   Focus On: The Vest Pocket Kodak   28

Chapter 5   The First World War   39

Chapter 6   Focus On: The Hythe Mark III Machine Gun
                Camera   82

Chapter 7   The Years Between the Wars   93

Chapter 8   Focus On: The Ensign Midget   113

Chapter 9   The Second World War   118

Chapter 10 Focus On: The Kodak Medalist   176

Chapter 11 The Cold War   187

Chapter 12 Focus On: The Minox   222

Chapter 13 The Korean War   232

Glossary of Photographic Terms   246
Bibliography   253
Picture Credits   254
Index   256

Introduction

There have been many books published on the subject of war photography. Typically they deal with the wars themselves or the difficulties of obtaining photographs in war zones, and they are illustrated with pictures of the military in action. This is not one of those books.

What we're looking at here are the cameras behind the pictures: the way the restrictions inherent in the use of early cameras influenced the kinds of pictures that could be taken; how easier ways of using later cameras changed the type of pictures that came out of wars; the ways in which wars shaped the design of cameras; the way cameras sometimes shaped

Wet plate sliding box cameras like this one made by the English company Horne and Thornthwaite were popular at the time of the Crimean War.

By the time of the Korean War, highly sophisticated Japanese 35mm cameras like this Nikon M had become favourites with press photographers.

the way a war was recorded; and the effect that wars had on cameras and photography in civilian life back on the home front during times of conflict.

The timeline covered in these pages is from the outbreak of the Crimean War in 1853 to the end of the Korean War in 1953, one hundred years in which cameras and photography came of age. At the start of that century of years, a photographer needed to be more of a scientist than an artist, such were the difficulties of shooting and processing any photograph. By the end, the latest cameras, with their compact dimensions, their versatility and ease of use, meant that photographers could largely forget the science and concentrate on the art.

This book will undoubtedly be read by photo historians who know how cameras operated but not how they were used in wars. But it will also be read by war historians who know little about the technicalities of how a camera works or is used. If that sounds like you, if you are someone who has little idea of what of an aperture is and how it is linked to shutter speeds, how depth of field is defined, the difference between a wide-angle

From a 1940s issue of *Camera Comics*: how Kodak advertised the part played by its cameras in the Second World War.

lens and a telephoto, or any other technical photographic term, don't despair. For you a glossary of photographic terms is included at the end of the book.

The types of cameras that went to war were many and varied. Some were already popular but now called into war service, others were adapted from already existing models, and there were cameras manufactured specially for specific wartime purposes. Some simply recorded events. Others defined and changed the way those events proceeded. War photographers are often lauded for their work, and rightly so. But it's worth remembering that behind all the great photographers, there were a lot of great cameras. This is their story.

A note about measurements

Today, the metric system of measuring in meters, centimetres and millimetres has largely taken over from the old imperial measurements that used yards, feet and inches. However, in the early days of photography, the imperial system was used more extensively than the metric system. For this reason, the following pages contain a mixture of metric and imperial measurement references. Straight descriptions of camera sizes are quoted in modern-day metric terms. But where equipment such as photographic plates or film sizes were originally made to imperial measurements, the original dimensions have been retained for historic accuracy.

Chapter 1

The Early Years

W hat is generally acknowledged to be the world's first photograph was taken by Frenchman Joseph Nicéphore Niépce in 1826. The process he used involved a pewter plate, coated with a substance called bitumen of Judea, and exposed in a device derived from a camera obscura, an aid employed by artists to project an image onto a screen in an effort to understand composition and perspective. At the

The camera used by Niépce to produce the first photograph. It would have been highly impractical for any form of war photography.

end of an all-day exposure in the adapted camera obscura, the bitumen had hardened and turned white where light had struck it. The remaining soft bitumen was then washed away with lavender oil and the base metal darkened by treatment with iodine vapour. Thus the highlights appeared white and the shadows were rendered black, producing a crude direct positive image. The camera and its associated image processing were somewhat impractical and their use in times of conflict could never have been feasible.

Daguerreotype cameras

The possibility of using cameras in wartime became viable, though not overly practical, with the announcement, in 1839, of the daguerreotype process. This first truly practical method of photography came courtesy of another Frenchman named Louis Jacques Mandé Daguerre. Because of the difficulty of using the process, daguerreotype cameras were employed mostly for studio work, when the subject of a portrait sat with his or her head held in a clamp to prevent movement during the necessarily long exposure times. Given that, it's difficult to believe that the resulting images, known as daguerreotypes, were ever made outside of a studio, let alone anywhere near a war zone. Consider what was involved merely to create a daguerreotype.

The photographer had to first make the plate on which the image would be recorded. For this, a copper sheet was coated with silver, then cleaned and polished using pumice and olive oil. Next, by the light of a candle, and in an airtight box, the plate was exposed to iodine crystals. The fumes combined with the silver on the plate to form a thin, light-sensitive layer of silver iodide. When the plate had taken on a golden-yellow colour it was exposed to bromine fumes to make it more sensitive, and was then ready for the camera.

Once the exposure had been made, the image had to be developed. Once again, using an airtight box, mercury was heated in a dish over a lamp. The exposed plate was then slotted face down into the box, allowing fumes to rise from the heated mercury and react with the silver iodide to form a white amalgam where light had struck the surface. The result was a positive image on a mirror-like silver surface.

The cameras that used this complicated process are best exemplified by considering Daguerre's own camera, made for him by his brother-in-law Alphonse Giroux, a French art restorer and cabinetmaker, with a lens made by Parisian optician and instrument maker Charles Chevalier. The camera was made of wood and comprised two boxes, one of which slid inside the other. The silver-plated copper plates on which its images were produced measured 6½ × 8½ inches, in imperial measurements, and that size thereafter became known as whole plate, one of the standard sizes for photographic images. The lens was a simple plano-convex design, which meant it was curved on one side and flat on the other. Its image was focused on a screen on the back of the camera by sliding the inner box,

The daguerreotype camera that introduced the first viable method of photography.

containing the focusing screen, backwards and forwards inside the outer box. A mirror was hinged to the back of the camera at 45 degrees, as an aid to the photographer who could look down into it to see a right-way-up image, as opposed to the upside-down image that the lens projected onto the focusing screen.

The shutter was no more than a flap across the lens that was moved to one side to make the exposure. Exposure time, due to the slow lenses and low sensitivity of the plates, ranged from a few seconds to several minutes. Because the daguerreotype process produced a direct positive with no intermediary negative to correct the lens's natural image, the picture was laterally reversed, unless a prism was placed on the front of the lens to correct it.

Later, daguerreotype cameras became more sophisticated, while better lenses meant exposure times could be reduced. But essentially, the overall process remained complicated and time-consuming. Even so, there is evidence of daguerreotypes being made during the Mexican-American War, an armed conflict between the two countries that was waged from 1846 to 1848. One of the earliest wartime photographs was taken in 1847 by an American daguerreotype photographer. It showed American troops riding into the Mexican city of Saltillo. Given the length of exposures in the daguerreotype process the photographer is likely to have persuaded the soldiers on horseback to stand as still as possible while the exposure was made. To the side of the image, a civilian looking out of a window and another walking away from the camera are both rendered slightly blurred because of their movement during the long exposure. During his time with the military, this now unknown photographer took pictures of army officers, Mexican civilians and battlefields. The restrictions of the process prevented him from capturing actual battles.

The calotype process

The daguerreotype process was followed by the calotype process, the brainchild of William Henry Fox Talbot – more generally known simply as Fox Talbot – who was an amateur scientist and Squire of the Manor in the English town of Lacock in Wiltshire. Initially, Fox Talbot's pictures were made by a process called photogenic drawing, in which the

Replica of one of Fox Talbot's cameras, used to produce the world's first negative.

image was exposed until it began to actually appear on sensitised paper, necessitating long exposure times. In 1835, four years before Daguerre's announcement, Fox Talbot used this process in a tiny camera to produce the world's first negative.

The scientist's experiments led him to a process that involved coating a sheet of paper with silver chloride, a chemical compound that is sensitive to light. When exposed in a suitable camera, the areas hit by light turned dark and the greater the intensity of the light, the darker the tone. In this way, a negative image was produced. When this was placed in contact with a second sheet of sensitised paper and exposed to light, the result was a contact print that showed a positive image.

Fox Talbot's significant breakthrough, one that would affect the future of photography, came about with the discovery of what was known as the latent image. It meant that the paper did not have to be exposed for the duration previously required for an image to appear. Instead, the paper could be removed from the camera sooner, even though it appeared there was no image on it. The negative image only appeared when the paper was developed in gallic acid, which accelerated the reaction of the silver chloride to light, and led to the formation of the previously invisible – or latent – image. Immediately exposure times were shortened. Once the image had been developed, it was then fixed in a solution of sodium hyposulfite, which negated its sensitivity to light to ensure it remained stable and became no darker when viewed in normal daylight.

In 1840, a year after Daguerre's announcement, Fox Talbot introduced his calotype process. It was the first time that a photographer had seen the importance of producing an intermediary negative, from which many positive images could be made, rather than producing a one-off direct positive image. It proved to be a photographic method that continued, in various forms, right up until the dawn of the digital age. Again, it was not a process that loaned itself readily to war photography, although there is evidence of calotypes being used to photograph military leaders in times of conflict. The cameras used to expose Fox Talbot's negatives followed the same kind of style used by daguerreotype photographers: a lens at the front, a holder for the paper negative at the back and a method of moving one in relation to the other to focus the image.

The next step forward was to coat the photographic emulsion onto glass. That resulted in more sensitive photographic plates, which led to more practical and faster shutter speeds. This in turn meant much shorter exposure times. Only then did taking cameras into war zones become truly practical for the first time, and the first conflict to be properly documented with this new method of photography was the Crimean War.

Chapter 2

The Crimean War

The Crimean War began in 1853 when Russia invaded the autonomous regions of Moldavia and Walachia, part of the Ottoman Empire that was strongly supported by British foreign policy. Britain was concerned for its merchant activity in the area. At the same time, along with France and Austria-Hungary, Britain regarded the Russian move as an expansionist threat. The war was fought from October 1853, although Britain and France didn't take part until 1854. It ended in February 1856, when Russia conceded defeat to the alliance of France, Britain, Sardinia and the Ottoman Empire.

With early forms of glass plate photography making the use of a camera in a war zone more practical than before, this became the first major conflict to be comprehensively documented by photography. Even so, the cameras and the processes needed to create actual images were far from easy to use.

Wet plate cameras

Two years before the outbreak of the Crimean War, photography on glass plates – a practice that continued well into the middle of the twentieth century – began with the wet collodion process. It was invented in 1851 by English artist, sculptor and photographer Frederick Scott Archer. Combined with the photographic emulsion he had formulated, the process cut exposure times drastically. Like the daguerreotype process before it, however, the wet collodion process was slow and awkward to use. Briefly, here's how it worked.

Before setting off, the photographer soaked cotton wool in a mixture of nitric and sulphuric acids, which when dry gave him guncotton. Dissolving this in a mixture of ether and alcohol produced collodion, with which he ventured forth with his camera, a set of clear glass plates and a mobile darkroom. On reaching his location, the photographer retired to his darkroom, where he washed one piece of glass in alcohol and powdered pumice. The previously made collodion, along with a solution of potassium iodide, was poured over the glass, ensuring that it covered it evenly. By the light of a candle, the plate was then lowered into a bath of silver nitrate and water. Removing it after a few minutes, it was ready to be inserted in the camera and used while wet. After exposure, the plate was returned to the darkroom where, still wet, it was developed with pyrogallic acid, fixed and washed. Prints were later made from the so produced glass negative using silver chloride or albumen printing paper. Mobile darkrooms, so necessary for the process to work, might be as small as a light-tight box on wheels, or as large as a horse-drawn wagon.

The cameras that used the wet plate process were mostly made of wood with the lens in a panel at the front and a plate holder at the rear. For focusing purposes, the lens was required to move backwards and

Made by A.T. Ottewill in 1851, a sliding box wet plate camera, a type that would have been used to record aspects of the Crimean War.

forwards in relation to the plate holder, and this movement was achieved in one of two ways. One method was to link the two parts of the camera with bellows, which folded like a concertina as the lens panel was moved back and forth. An alternative style involved two boxes in which a box slid inside a slightly larger box, with a lens at the front of one and the plate holder at the back of the other. The back of the camera also incorporated a ground-glass focusing screen, which could be removed or set aside for the insertion of the plate holder. Images on the focusing screen were rendered upside down by the lens and were viewed by the photographer with his head under a large hood made of lightproof cloth. In most wet plate cameras, the lens contained apertures, which either dropped into place via a slot in the lens barrel, or were on a rotating disc. Exposure was made, not with a shutter as would be the norm in later cameras, but by simply removing a cap over the lens and then quickly replacing it.

A typical shooting sequence would go like this:

1. Set the camera up on a tripod.
2. Remove the lens cap and focus the image on the ground-glass screen.
3. Replace the lens cap.
4. Retire to the mobile darkroom and prepare the plate.
5. Place the prepared plate in its holder while still wet and cover it with a slide-in dark slide to prevent light reaching the sensitive surface before exposure.
6. Exchange the camera's focusing screen for the plate holder containing the newly made, wet photographic plate.
7. Remove the dark slide so that the plate's sensitive surface faced the capped lens.
8. Remove and replace the lens cap to make the exposure.
9. Replace the dark slide and remove the plate holder from the camera.
10. Back in the mobile darkroom, remove the plate from its holder and process it.

Given the complications of the camera use, plate preparation and development, it is difficult to image how any photographer would even think of entering a war zone to shoot pictures. In fact, there is only a little evidence of wet plate cameras being used during actual conflict.

Another sliding box wet plate camera from this era, made by Dallmeyer to shoot 6 × 6-inch pictures.

But for photographing the aftermath of battles, battlefields and military personnel, the process was used extensively, in a way that recorded war subjects with methods never before attempted.

The man considered to be the world's first combat photographer was Carol Szathmari, a Hungarian who took his wet plate camera to the Crimean War, where he shot more than 200 images, none of which have survived today. Richard Nicklin, a civilian professional photographer, along with two assistants, was also commissioned to shoot military installations at the start of the war. In 1854, he set off for Varna, a nucleus for Anglo-French forces, and was never heard of again. Both of these photographers were early exponents of war photography, whose work is largely unknown today. But, when it comes to the use of wet plate photography and ways in which it documented the Crimean War, one name stands above all others.

Roger Fenton

The son of a wealthy, northern England industrialist, Fenton was a painter before he became a photographer, studying as a pupil of French artist Paul Delaroche, famous for painting historical scenes. But Delaroche was also interested in early photographic processes, exclaiming when he saw his first daguerreotype, 'From today, painting is dead.' His interests obviously rubbed off on his pupil and, even though Fenton went on to study law and practise as a solicitor, he retained an interest in photography and was a user of Fox Talbot's calotype process. He also became a founder member and secretary of the Photographic Society, later to become the Royal Photographic Society, which was formed in 1853 and remains active today. After a visit to Russia in 1852, where he photographed the Kremlin, Fenton became a full-time professional photographer, famous for landscape and portrait work and he even photographed the Royal Family. With the outbreak of the Crimean War, he was paid by the British government to act as an official campaign photographer.

Because the wet collodion process was then the best method of photography, Fenton needed to take not only cameras, but also a darkroom with him. His darkroom on wheels prepared for the purpose was converted from a wine merchant's horse-drawn vehicle. It was fitted with yellow window panes and shutters, a tank of water and racks to hold the various dishes and chemicals needed for the preparation and development of the wet plates. It also contained his bed and washing facilities.

After a photographic trial run around Yorkshire to ensure everything worked as it should, Fenton left England, along with his mobile darkroom and two assistants, bound for the Crimean War in 1855, acquiring three horses to draw his van along the way. The equipment he took included 700 glass plates and five cameras, of which the largest was capable of shooting huge 16×20-inch wet plate negatives. During his travels, he shot around 350 pictures.

With exposure times running at between three and twenty seconds in the brightest light, and even though Fenton personally witnessed the horrors of the war, the limitations of the wet plate process prevented him from capturing actual battle action. Neither was that a requirement. He

Photographed during the Crimean War, Roger Fenton's assistant Marcus Sparling sitting on Fenton's mobile horse-drawn darkroom.

was, after all, contracted by the British government, who preferred for him not to show the public back home the horrors of war, but images that would placate rather than shock them.

So his photographs consisted mostly of landscapes, the locations of battlefields post-battle, portraits of British Army officers and life in the military camps, many of which had to be carefully posed and entailed the subjects standing very still during the lengthy exposure times to prevent them recording as blurred images. As the war ended, public interest in the conflict rapidly faded. Fenton gave up photography in 1862 and died a few years later, largely forgotten. Today, he is recognised as one of the earliest professional war photographers, his work famous, not just for his keen artistic eye, but also in recognition of the complications of using the wet plate process in such difficult situations.

Other Crimean War photographers

Fenton became the most famous of the wet plate photographers to cover the Crimean War, but he was by no means the only one. The later stages of the war were also photographed by James Robertson, an English gem and coin engraver who moved on to become Superintendant and Chief Engraver for the Imperial Mint in Constantinople. Like Fenton, he was unable to shoot scenes of real action, but was adept at recording the scenes leading up to and the aftermath of the battles. He shot about sixty pictures in all. French photographer Charles Langlois was also responsible for photographing the war, though his pictures today are virtually unknown.

Matthew Brady

Meanwhile in America, in 1860, an itinerant portrait painter named Matthew Brady came to fame with the advent of the wet plate process, which he used to photograph Abraham Lincoln. In 1861, Brady, having won the admiration of Lincoln, who put his election down partly to at least one of the thirty or so pictures the photographer took of him, was offered the president's personal authorisation to travel with the Union during the American Civil War. He travelled alongside a small band of other hired photographers, complete with cameras, mobile studio and darkroom. He and his team even managed to capture some real battles, and became famous for taking their cameras into the thick of the action whenever they could. He was, however, known more for staging scenes with troops willing to pose to simulate the action. Some of his most iconic images showed battlefields strewn with the bodies of the dead, although it later transpired that he might have repositioned some of the bodies for maximum visual effect.

Although his actions might seem like cheating, they brought home to the public a perception of the war that might have been otherwise difficult to visualise, and really, were his staged photographs so very different to other pictures of the war drawn, with a certain amount of licence, by artists for illustrations in periodicals like *The Illustrated London News*? Brady was also known for his portraits of famous military personnel from the war, captured by his camera in a mobile studio.

As the war went on, Brady spent more time back home in Washington overseeing his teams of photographers, although he did return to the front from time to time and often came under fire.

Brady personally financed his work to the tune of about $100,000, at one time employing as many as twenty photographers in the field. He was later partly compensated by the United States government, who gave him around a quarter of his outlay, but it wasn't enough to keep him from bankruptcy. He died penniless in 1896.

In 1871, fifteen years after the Crimean War ended and six years after the end of the American Civil War, the inconveniences of the wet plate photographic process were replaced by the far more convenient use of dry plates. It was too late for pioneers like Szathmari, Fenton, Robertson, Langlois and Brady, but life was about to get a lot easier for the next generation of war photographers.

Chapter 3

Cameras and Photography in 1914

Between the end of the Crimean War in 1856 and the start of the First World War in 1914, photography came of age, as early experiments and false starts in the processes that initially produced images coalesced into one single procedure in which a negative was first produced, from which numerous positive prints could be made. Although that fundamental process was adopted by a great many different shapes, styles and sizes of camera, they all came down to just two basic types: cameras in which the initial negatives were made on rigid glass plates, and cameras whose negatives were made on rolls of flexible film. Both would come to be used in wartime photography, for different purposes, in battle and on the home front.

Glass plate cameras

Photography on glass plates, which had begun with the complicated wet collodion process, became far more practical with the advent of dry plates. They were the invention of English physician Richard Leach Maddox and were made by suspending light-sensitive silver bromide in an emulsion of gelatine, which was then coated onto glass, the process of course taking place in the dark. The big advantage was that plates could be manufactured in advance, kept until needed to take a picture and developed at a later date. Suddenly mobile darkrooms became a thing of the past. Dry plates first appeared in 1871. By 1878, photographic dry plates were being mass produced in purpose-built factories.

The advantages of using dry plates over wet plates didn't end with their convenience of use. Dry plates were about sixty times more sensitive than the old wet collodion plates. For the first time, shutter speeds could be measured in fractions of a second, rather than full seconds or even minutes. Without the need to hold the camera perfectly still during the

Eastman No.3 Plate Camera, a dry plate model that was available around the turn of the twentieth century.

previously long exposures, it could now be freed from its tripod and handheld. Shutters with adjustable speeds began to be produced, first as add-on accessories, but soon to be incorporated into the design of every new model of camera.

Cameras that had before been traditionally made of wood, very often the products of cabinetmakers rather than bespoke camera manufacturers, started to be produced in metal, frequently with leather covering. With the new sensitivity of the plates, it was no longer necessary to build large lenses to gather as much light as possible. Lenses grew smaller, and so too did the camera bodies to which they were attached.

The most popular cameras of the time, ironically given what was about to transpire, were made in England and Germany. By far the most prolific

Add-on shutters like this one made by the English company Lancaster in 1885 freed up the camera from the rigidity of a tripod. It worked by the use of a rubber band.

By 1914, plate cameras like this Goerz Vest-Pocket Tenax had become smaller and could be folded to fit into a pocket.

The Special Sibyl camera, made by the English company Newman and Guardia, a typical metal bodied folding plate camera on sale in 1914.

design was for folding bellows cameras, made for various sizes of plate, measured in those days in imperial measurements, from $2\frac{1}{2} \times 3\frac{1}{2}$ inches up to 8×10 inches. Although many styles of camera proliferated, the basic concept remained much the same: a lens in a panel on the front, linked by bellows to a plate holder in the back. When not in use, the camera could be folded. A typical style might involve the lens panel being pushed back along the baseboard to meet the plate holder back, and the whole thing folded down on hinges to make a flat package. In another design, the lens panel retracted to meet the back panel inside a shallow box.

Operation of the camera was much the same as in wet plate days. The holder with a photographic plate in it was placed into the camera back in place of the ground-glass screen on which the image had been focused, the dark slide removed from the holder, the exposure made using a shutter rather than removing and replacing a cap, the dark slide replaced and the plate holder removed.

With the fast adoption of dry plates, another type of camera also began to grow in popularity around this time. The singe lens reflex still used a lens that focused on a photographic plate in the back of the camera as usual, with the same manipulation of the plate holder and dark slide as the picture was taken. The difference with this new type of camera lay in the viewfinder. Where previously the lens's image had been focused on a screen on the back of the camera body, the single lens reflex added a mirror behind the lens to interrupt the light path and reflect its image up to a screen under a hood on top of the body. As the exposure was made, the mirror flipped up and out of the way of the lens's light path, allowing its image to then register on the photographic plate at the back of the camera. This gave three advantages:

1. The photographer could preview the picture right up to the instant the exposure was made.
2. Because of the optical path of the light via a mirror, the image was seen on the viewfinder screen the right way up, instead of upside down as was the case with a focusing screen at the back of the camera.
3. The plate holder could be inserted and left in place during focusing and picture composition, rather than waiting until both actions were completed before swapping the screen for the plate holder.

Single lens reflexes came in many different shapes and sizes, and a great many of them were made to fold when not in use in complicated and ingenious ways.

Photography on glass plates, using these two types of camera, remained popular with professional photographers until as late as the 1950s, and

The Fallowflex camera, a typical single lens reflex on sale in 1914.

these were the cameras that largely documented the coming war. But side-by-side with plate cameras, a new technology was quietly evolving that used rolls of flexible film in place of solid glass plates.

Roll film cameras

The American George Eastman, at the time a junior clerk in the Rochester Savings Bank, was the pioneering force behind the idea of shooting pictures on rolls of flexible film, rather than on rigid glass plates. He was a keen amateur photographer, who began by using the wet plate process. As Eastman became more interested in photography he started to look at ways to make the process simpler and he began experimenting with manufacturing his own dry plates. At first he did this only for his own use, but soon saw the commercial possibilities of making and selling his plates. For three years, he worked at the bank during the day and carried out experiments in his mother's kitchen at night. In 1880, he took out a lease on business premises in Rochester and began making dry plates as a commercial venture. That was when he began looking in another direction. If an emulsion could be permanently coated onto glass, why not something more flexible, like paper?

After some experimentation, which included making a film in which the emulsion had to be stripped from its paper base during development, Eastman turned his attention to coating the photographic emulsion onto celluloid. It marked the start of roll film photography, which continued in various incarnations right up until the digital age.

In 1888, along with his new film, Eastman launched a camera called the Kodak. It was the first time that now well-known name had been used. The word was Eastman's own invention. He had a liking for the letter K and from that constructed a word that began and ended with the letter. Writing about it to the British Patent Office, he said: 'It has the following merits as a trademark. It is short. It is not capable of mispronunciation. It does not resemble anything in the art and cannot be associated with anything else in the art.'

Until then, photography had been a complicated and expensive business, very much the province of professional or very keen amateur photographers. Eastman's Kodak, for the first time, was aimed at people

The Kodak was the first roll film camera.

who might never before have thought of owning a camera. The word 'snapshot' had hitherto referred only to a gunshot fired quickly, without seriously aiming, at a fast-moving target that might suddenly present itself. But now the word took on a new meaning. Snapshot photography for the masses had arrived with a camera that made the whole process of shooting pictures and developing the images easier than ever before.

The camera was a box type, certainly not the first box-shaped camera, but undoubtedly a significant influence on the shape of things to come, as far as the snapshot market was concerned. The Kodak measured

16 × 8 × 9cm, weighed just 900 grams and was covered in black morocco leather. It had only three controls: a string to tension the shutter, a button to release it and a key to wind the film. It was purchased ready-loaded with enough film for 100 exposures. When they had all been shot, the camera and film together were returned to the Eastman works for developing and printing, where the prints were made from negatives, contact-printed by daylight in batches of twelve, then mounted together before being cut into individual prints. The camera was reloaded with a new film and returned to the photographer. Five days after that, the owner received the prints, mounted and burnished, together with the negatives, for the sum of two guineas (£2 2s, or £2.10 decimal equivalent). The first camera sold in the UK for five guineas (£5 5s or £5.25) and in the US for $25.

In the years that followed, Eastman launched new and larger versions of the Kodak. In 1900, by which time amateurs as well as professionals were developing their own film, the Eastman works introduced the first

The original Brownie from Kodak.

Brownie camera and followed it the next year with the number two version, which took a film size called 120. Modified and updated versions of that size remained popular until the advent of digital cameras, and can still be purchased today by enthusiasts who enjoy using older film equipment. It was initially used in cameras to take 6 × 9cm negatives.

Eastman wasn't just an inventor; he was also a brilliant marketeer, who soon saw the advantage of allowing other camera manufacturers to make their own roll film cameras, whose users would have to return to Eastman to buy their film. In the years ahead, a great many different styles and sizes of roll film cameras were made for varying negative sizes. By the time the First World War broke out, roll film proliferated, used in both purpose-made cameras, and also in special film backs that could be attached to plate cameras in place of their usual glass plate holders.

Despite this, professional photographers who were about to begin documenting the war mostly stuck to their large format plate cameras. But many amateur photographers who signed up for action, much against all the rules and regulations, took roll film cameras into battle with them.

Movie cameras

The First World War might not have been the very first to be documented by photographers, but it was the first in which movie footage was extensively shot.

The man most often credited with being the first to produce a movie camera is the American inventor Thomas Edison, who announced a camera called the Kinetograph in 1893. His announcement, however, was predated by several other movie pioneers. They included the English inventor William Freese-Greene, whose gravestone in London's Highgate Cemetery is inscribed with the words 'The inventor of Kinematography'. He demonstrated a crude form of movie photography in 1885 by projecting a series of images shot on reels of paper. English barrister and political activist Wordsworth Donisthorpe demonstrated moving pictures shot on sensitised strips of celluloid in 1889, and a brief snippet of film showing moving images of London's Trafalgar Square in 1890 still exists.

Edison, however, unlike some of the pioneers before him, was already famous as an inventor, eventually responsible for more than 1,000 inventions during his lifetime, and it was his voice that was heard most strongly in association with the invention of the movie camera. His early experiments had led him to producing moving images by placing a series of images on a sensitised rotating cylinder, but inspiration truly struck when he heard about George Eastman's Kodak. The celluloid film used in Eastman's camera seemed to Edison to be exactly what he needed to make movie film. Eastman's film was 70mm wide, but Edison cut it in half to run

An unnamed hand-cranked wooden movie camera of the time, made to shoot 35mm film.

through his kinetograph, and 35mm became the standard gauge for movie cameras.

Moving pictures from the kinetograph were not projected onto a screen for viewing. Instead, they were viewed in a separate piece of apparatus called a Kinetoscope, which could be viewed by only one person a time. It wasn't until brothers Auguste and Louis Lumière in France produced the first movie projectors that moving pictures became available for viewing by large audiences.

Throughout the early 1900s, movie camera and projector technology steadily progressed until, by 1914, cameras were readily available for shooting moving pictures on 35mm film, to be shown later on a suitable projector.

A typical movie camera of the time would have taken the form of a large box with lens on the front and a handle on the side. Cranking the handle at a steady rate wound the film from one spool to another behind the lens. The most popular method of moving the film through the camera was with a ratchet arrangement originally inspired by the movement of the needle in a sewing machine. The film was perforated and, as the handle was turned, the ratchet reached up, grabbed the film by one of its perforations and pulled it down to a position behind the lens. As it came to a brief rest, the shutter mechanism, also behind the lens, allowed through light to expose one frame before the ratchet reached up and pulled the next piece of film into position. So the finished film was made up of a series of still pictures shot in sequence. Once developed, the film travelled through a projector, showing the series of pictures, one immediately following the other, each with a slightly different view of the same scene. In theory, the viewer should have seen a series of fast-moving still images, but because of a phenomenon of the human eye called persistence of vision, one image was momentarily retained, during which time the next replaced it. So what the eye actually perceived was one long moving picture.

And so to war

By 1914, both still and movie photography were big business right across the civilised world. The *British Journal Photographic Almanac*, published annually to review the latest photographic trends and equipment, produced a bumper issue of 1,496 pages that year, more than three-quarters of which comprised advertising for the latest products. Still photography and movie camera manufacturers mentioned included Adams, Butchers, Fallowfield, Newman and Guardia, Sanderson, Shew and Thornton Pickard, alongside German makers such as Goerz, Contessa, Voigtländer and Zeiss, with photographic plates and printing paper made by the likes of Barnet, Ilford, Paget and Wellington. Other makers of cameras, photographic material and various sundries came from America, Australia, France, India, Japan and more. Cameras and photography, it seemed, knew no boundaries, as international manufacturers worldwide came together to make and sell their products to professional photographers and keen amateurs alike.

And then the world went to war. Nations that had previously been bound by photography, both as manufacturers and as camera users, became enemies overnight. But they went to war, and they took their cameras with them, irrespective of whether those cameras had been made by friend or foe.

Chapter 4

Focus On: The Vest Pocket Kodak

O ne camera, more than any other, became synonymous with unofficial photography during the First World War. Unofficial because, while there were professional photographers with large format professional cameras recording the war, soldiers who were also amateur photographers, much against the rules, were taking their

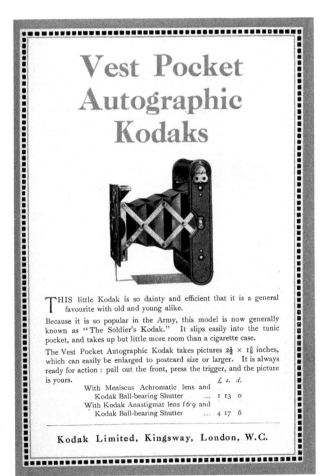

How the Vest Pocket Kodak was advertised, with reference to its use as 'the soldier's camera'.

own cameras into battle. To serve that purpose, the camera needed to be unobtrusive, with a technical specification good enough to produce reasonably sized, quality pictures, and small enough to be hidden in a tunic pocket. All of those criteria were met by the Vest Pocket Kodak. Launched in 1912, two years before the First World War broke out, it was the conflict that gave the camera a nickname, which came about in 1915 when Kodak marketed it as The Soldier's Camera.

Introduction of the camera

The word 'vest' in the context of the camera name was the American word for what, in Britain, is more popularly known as a waistcoat. The genesis of the Vest Pocket Kodak began at the end of the nineteenth century and the early years of the twentieth. Until then, the most common shape for a Kodak camera had been an inflexible box. Then came the launch of a series of cameras that fell under the general name of Folding Pocket Kodaks, which unfolded in various ways for use with the lens in a panel that sat at the end of flexible bellows. The most common style of this type was shaped, when folded, like a flat box, from which a bed folded down. The lens, on its bellows, was pulled out along this bed on rails. Despite the fact this made the cameras more portable than before, the overall dimensions when folded were still large, not the kind of size that could fit comfortably into a pocket.

The Vest Pocket Kodak in its folded position.

The Vest Pocket Kodak open and ready for action.

What made the Vest Pocket Kodak smaller and more likely to fit easily into a vest, or waistcoat, pocket was the introduction by Kodak, at the same time as the camera, of a new film size called 127, coupled with a different method of folding. In its folded position, the camera measured a mere 12 × 6 × 2.5cm. Tugging on small finger grips each side of the body allowed the lens panel to extend on bellows, supported by scissor-like struts, increasing the width of the body from 2.5cm to 10cm. The camera was the star of Kodak's 1912 catalogue of new and current equipment. Here's what it had to say.

> No matter how many cameras you have, there are times when a vest pocket edition of your larger instrument will be appreciated. That's just what the Vest Pocket Kodak is – a miniature Kodak – so flat and smooth and small as to go readily into a vest pocket, so carefully made as to be capable of the highest grade of work. Quality marks the Vest Pocket Kodak in every detail. It is not made small so that we can produce a cheap camera; it is made small simply for the sake of convenience. The small price is simply the result of our manufacturing facilities.

The price when launched in America was $6, approximately £1 5s (£1.25) in the UK, according to dollar-to-pound exchange rates in 1912 and translating pre-decimal currency to current decimal coinage. This was at a time when a second lieutenant in the infantry earned 7s 6d (approximately 37p) a day and a lieutenant-colonel earned £1 8s (£1.40) a day.

Autographic versions

In 1914, new versions of already established Kodak folding cameras began to appear, thanks to Henry Gaisman, the inventor of the safety razor. The rolls of film used in both the Vest Pocket Kodak and the larger cameras were attached to backing paper that was slightly longer than the film itself with a leader and a trailer at each end. Because the backing paper was lightproof, film could be loaded into the camera in daylight, the back closed and then wound until the light-sensitive film was in position for the first exposure. The backing paper also contained numbers, which, read through a red window in the back of the camera, indicated when each frame was in the correct position for the next exposure. The window was coloured red because film of the day was insensitive to red light and therefore would not be fogged by light entering the camera through the window.

Gaisman's invention was for a new type of autographic film, in which the backing paper was not completely lightproof, but with an intermediary sheet of lightproof carbon paper placed between backing paper and film. The back of the camera that used the new type of film contained a small trapdoor and a stylus usually, but not always, attached to it.

How the autographic trapdoor was opened, with the stylus used for writing details to be exposed onto the film.

As each picture was taken, the trapdoor was opened and the stylus used to write on the backing paper. If the photographer applied just the right amount of pressure, it made only an indentation in the backing paper, but broke the surface of the carbon paper beneath. The trapdoor was then left open and exposed to light for a few seconds. The result was that the writing on the carbon was exposed onto the film in the rebate between each negative. In this way, the photographer could record the location, exposure details or any other brief amounts of information onto the film for reference later when the negatives were used to make prints.

In 1914, George Eastman, the man who founded Kodak, paid $300,000 to Gaisman for the right to use his invention on Kodak cameras, which he termed Autographic Kodaks. The style was first used in 1915, when the Vest Pocket Kodak became known as the Vest Pocket Autographic Kodak.

In this way, soldiers who took their cameras to war could record brief information about each of the pictures they took directly onto the film, beside each appropriate negative. Information so recorded was usually a date and perhaps an indication of the location, although often codes were used or letters left out of place names for reasons of security.

By now there were three models of the camera available, each with a better lens, with prices ranging from $6 to $22.50, which, at 1914 exchange rates, equated then to £1 5s to £4 14s. In that year, Kodak's catalogue described new versions of the camera thus:

For average work this little Kodak fitted with a tested meniscus lens produces excellent pictures under all ordinary conditions. For microscopic definition and clearness of details, the Kodak Anastigmat lens has proven a great success. This lens offers the usual advantages of anastigmat equipment at a surprisingly low price. It works at a speed of f/7.7 and is fully corrected. Then for those who want not only the absolute sharpness and flatness of field of the anastigmat, but the maximum speed as well, we fit the camera with a Zeiss Kodak Anastigmat f/6.9 lens.

The Vest Pocket Autographic Kodak is built as accurately as a watch and the Kodak Ball Bearing shutter, which is supplied with all three lens equipments, works with precision and without jerk or jar. Although made of metal, the camera is light in weight and extremely

An advertisement for the Vest Pocket Enlarging Camera that enabled larger prints to be made from the camera's small negatives.

Signalize some of your Kodak masterpieces

with a

Vest Pocket Kodak or Brownie Enlarging Camera

That very interest or beauty that made the picture a master-piece in its regular size will be accentuated in the large print. And with the Brownie Enlarging Camera successful large prints are not a matter of ability but a matter of course.

No focusing—no dark-room. Just slip in your negative at one end of the camera, your Velox paper at the other, expose by daylight and develop and fix in the regular way.

THE PRICE.

V. P. Kodak Enlarging Camera, for 3¼ x 5½ enlargements from 1⅝ x 2½ negatives, - - - - - - - -	$1.75
No. 2 Brownie Post Card Enlarging Camera, for 3¼ x 5½ enlargements from 2¼ x 3¼ negatives, - - - - -	1.75
No. 2 Brownie Enlarging Camera, for 5 x 7 enlargements from 2¼ x 3¼ negatives, - - - - - - -	2.00
No. 3 ditto, for 6½ x 8½ enlargements from 3¼ x 4¼ negatives, -	3.00
No. 4 ditto, for 8 x 10 enlargements from 4 x 5 negatives (will also take 3¼ x 5½ negatives), - - - - - -	4.00

CANADIAN KODAK CO., LIMITED
TORONTO, CANADA.

At Your Dealer's.

compact. It is always ready for action as it is only necessary to pull out the front to its full extent and it is focused at any distance. It has a brilliant reversible viewfinder.

The Vest Pocket Kodak cameras took eight pictures to a roll of 127 size film. In the imperial measurements used in those days, the negative size was $1\frac{5}{8} \times 2\frac{1}{2}$ inches. The negatives could be used to make enlarged prints in a normal darkroom, or enlarged to postcard size in the portable Vest Pocket Kodak Enlarging Camera.

The camera in action

The Vest Pocket Kodak won the respect of its soldier users, not just for its portability, but equally for its ease of use, even by those who were not experienced amateur photographers. Because the lens was fixed focus, there was no need to adjust it for camera-to-subject distances. Providing the photographer did not get too close to his subject, the picture would be sharp from a few feet away to infinity.

The exposure guide engraved beneath the lens of the camera.

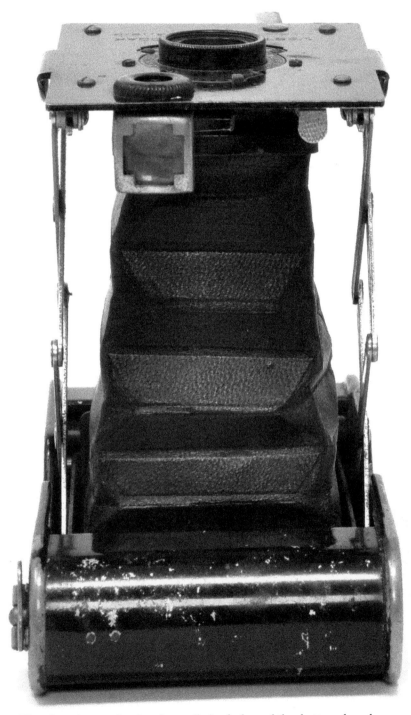

View from the top, showing the small viewfinder and the shutter release lever.

The camera had only two shutter speeds of 1/25 and 1/50 second to worry about, and the apertures, although designated by the usual f-stops, were also described by engravings beneath the lens with reference to certain types of subject. From the smallest aperture to the largest, the descriptions ran: *marine clouds snow, distant view, average view, near view, portrait, moving objects.* The shutter speed and aperture settings could be adjusted before opening the camera. Then the finger grips on each side were pulled to extend the lens, the view composed by squinting into a very small viewfinder at the top of the lens panel, the shutter released by pressing a lever opposite the viewfinder and the film wound by a key on the end of the body until the next number appeared in the red window on the back, indicating that the camera was ready for the next exposure.

Soldiers with their unofficial Vest Pocket Kodaks in their tunic pockets were in a position to capture scenes of war, or perhaps landmarks soon to be destroyed, in a way that the professional photographer away from action might have missed, and they could capture the human element of the war from right in its midst in a way that might not otherwise have come to the attention of those at home.

Although the War Office frowned on the use of cameras during the war, very little was done to check what soldiers of all ranks were carrying in the form of photographic equipment. As early as Christmas 1914, the British Army issued a General Routine Order, stating that the taking of pictures was not permitted, the sending of film through the post was prohibited and anyone contravening those rules would be arrested.

Yet pictures continued to be taken and leaked back home to the British press. Despite the difficulties and prohibitions, amateur photographers among soldiers of all ranks continued to document the war with pictures of life in the trenches, battlefields and even the famous Christmas truce of 1914 when British and German soldiers emerged from their trenches on Christmas Day to exchange cigarettes and chocolate, to chat as best they could in their different languages and to even play football against one another. For a time the Christmas truce story was thought to be a myth. But soldiers' pictures, taken at the time, proved otherwise.

An article in the June 1915 issue of *Kodakery*, a magazine produced by Kodak for its customers, headed *The Part of the Kodak at the Front*, spoke of the prominent place Kodak cameras were taking as historians of the war, and continued:

Thousands of Kodaks are in the knapsacks of officers and soldiers in all the armies engaged, and when the smoke of battle has been cleared away, their tiny films will have a war story to tell – to us and to posterity – such as has never been told before.

Although there were undoubtedly other cameras around, the ease of use and its convenient size meant that a good proportion of those pictures were shot with a Vest Pocket Kodak – also known as the soldier's camera.

Chapter 5

The First World War

When the world went to war in 1914, amateur and professional photographers of every nation set out to document the events; and not only the war was captured on film, but also its cause. The assassination of Archduke Franz Ferdinand in Sarajevo on 28 June 1914 is generally accepted as the pivotal episode that triggered hostilities. Photographs taken on that fateful day, and soon published around the world, went a long way towards stirring up the patriotic fervour that brought so many nations, with their alliances to one another, into the war so quickly.

Walter Tausch was the professional photographer who took pictures at the scene of the assassination. He was an Austrian photographer who, in 1910, had moved to Sarajevo to open a studio and who was there on that day to cover the visit of the archduke and his wife, little realising that the pictures he was about to take would have such an important part to play in world history.

At the start of the war, photography was considered to be a luxury pastime and one that was doomed to suffer, perhaps even to become extinct, as much of the materials needed for manufacturing photographic goods came from what were now enemy nations. In fact, the opposite happened. As photography proved itself to be an invaluable tool for reconnaissance, ways and means were found to find and manufacture the raw materials at home and it was suggested that, after the war, Britain would no longer be reliant on foreign photographic resources.

Photography played its part too in the field of propaganda, as neutral and allied countries began to see for the first time photographic evidence of the devastation caused by the war.

There had never before been a war that was so well documented by photography. Hundreds of thousands of pictures were taken during the various conflicts, and yet one of the biggest battles for photographers was the fight against censorship. With the advent of smaller and easier-to-use cameras, photography from the battle fronts was now possible, even though it was not officially permissible. Back home, the public saw next to nothing when it came to pictures of the true horrors of the war. Civilian photographers were not allowed anywhere near the front. The penalty for soldiers who were there fighting and were caught sneaking out their Vest Pocket Kodaks and the like to take a picture or two was arrest and, reputedly, death. When a small selection of army officers were officially sanctioned to photograph the Western Front, their photographs were for record purposes only, not for consumption by the public via newspapers or magazines.

Apart from access to a small sampling of officially sanctioned pictures, newspaper and magazine editors who needed to illustrate stories of the war had to content themselves with images that showed a general representation of the story being covered, or even an artist's line drawing, rather than photographs of actual events. And they were not happy about it. In protest, newspaper and magazine editors, together with picture agencies, came together to form the Proprietors' Association of Press Photographic Agencies in an effort to negotiate with the government to allow civilian photographers to cover the action at the front. They didn't get their way as far as civilian photographers were concerned, but the government did appoint official war photographers. For this purpose they chose military personnel who had worked as newspaper photographers in their civilian lives. The pictures they produced were rarely dramatic and more likely to show columns of soldiers on the march, or posing for the camera in their camps, eating or cleaning their guns. Because the photographer had time to arrange his shots, they were often technically perfect and imaginatively composed, obeying all the traditional rules of picture composition.

One famous picture by Ernest Brooks, the first official photographer to be appointed by the British military, showed soldiers, loaded down with guns and backpacks, in silhouette against a dramatic sky as they picked their way across the landscape. To shoot a picture like this, Brooks would have had to understand the nuances of correct exposure. If he had simply shot the five soldiers with more traditional detail in their faces and clothing, then the sky would have been over-exposed and recorded as

Ernest Brooks's evocative picture of silhouetted soldiers.

pure white. But by adjusting exposure for the sky itself, the figures were under-exposed, rendering them only as silhouettes, which nevertheless were immediately identifiable as soldiers. In another of his photographs, hundreds of troops were seen trekking along a road that wound through a barren landscape. Photographed, looking down from an elevated position, the road and troops made a perfect 'S' shape that led the eye from foreground to background in one of the classic pictorial picture compositions.

This latter picture is the kind of thing that the photographer could have simply come by and been ready to shoot, whereas the silhouetted soldiers against the sky might easily have been posed. In fact, history has shown that war photographers were not averse to setting up pictures in this way and posing their subjects to recreate scenes that they might have witnessed earlier and been unable to photograph 'live'. In 1916, Britain introduced the Propaganda of Facts policy, which banned images faked in this way. It should have prevented the practice for good, but it probably didn't.

Camera usage

Plate cameras of this time were big, heavy, unwieldy and complicated to use, contributing largely to the reason why so many pictures taken were of static subjects like soldiers in camp, rather than in the thick of battle.

Photography has always been a mixture of art and science. Today, much of the science is handled by the camera automatically. In the early days it was very different. A photographer needed to be an artist in order to arrange his pictures for the most pleasing composition, even when the subject itself in wartime might have been anything but pleasing. But then the science side kicked in.

First there was the matter of getting the exposure correct for the amount of light falling on the subject, depending on the time of day and weather conditions. This was achieved by juggling shutter speeds and lens apertures. Shutter speeds, measured in fractions of a second, controlled the amount of time light was allowed to pass through the lens. Apertures, which were represented by an opening that could be varied in size behind the lens, controlled the intensity of the light. Bright weather conditions required small apertures and fast shutter speeds; low light meant using wide apertures and slow speeds. But the shutter speed also controlled the way action was recorded. If a picture contained a lot of movement, it required a faster shutter speed to prevent blurring the subject, and a faster shutter speed, which reduced the time light fell through the lens, demanded a wider aperture to increase the intensity of the light.

Later, electronic exposure meters would be invented to relay the correct information to the photographer; later still, cameras would have built-in exposure meters to give similar information and even adjust the exposure automatically. But no such thing existed in the 1914–18 period of the First World War. The photographer might have had a printed table that gave him suggested combinations of shutter speeds and apertures for different degrees of light, but much of the information was subjective. Faced with a table entry that gave a suggested exposure for when the weather was 'cloudy but bright', how was the photographer to ascertain just how bright was bright?

There were primitive forms of exposure meter that could be employed. Photometers, for example, were devices that a photographer could look into through an eyepiece to compare the ambient light with a standard inbuilt light source. But since that standard light source was likely to have been a candle, it wasn't the most ideal of contraptions to be using in the field. A better bet for a photographer of those days was use of another type of exposure meter known as an actinometer. These were about the size and shape of a small pocket watch, into which a piece of light-sensitive paper was inserted. The length of time it took for the paper to darken enough to match a standard tint built into the meter gave the photographer a basis for calculating exposure. The Watkins Bee Meter was a typical example. Introduced in the 1890s, it was still being used during the time of the First World War.

Watkins Bee Meter, popular with photographers at the time of the First World War as an aid to setting correct exposures.

All of this was time-consuming and unlikely to be welcomed in a scenario in which pictures might suddenly present themselves with a need to be photographed at a moment's notice. The upshot was that experienced photographers developed an uncanny instinct for recognising light levels and translating them into shutter speed and aperture combinations in their heads.

An upside-down image of the subject was projected onto a plate camera's ground-glass focusing screen.

So much for exposure. But then came focusing. The lens needed to be set at an accurate distance measured from the camera to the principal subject. Most plate cameras incorporated a ground-glass focusing screen at the rear on which the lens projected an upside-down image of the subject, viewed by the photographer with his head under a dark cloth. In this way the image was composed and then focused by movement of the lens. Prior to exposure the screen was removed and replaced by the photographic plate.

Roll film cameras didn't have the luxury of a focusing screen, and needed other ways to measure and set focusing distances. The No.3A Autographic Kodak Special was the first camera with a coupled rangefinder, an optical device to measure camera-to-subject distance. But, although that camera was launched in 1916, the idea was slow to catch on, and rangefinders were not available in the types of cameras used by war photographers of this era. There were primitive distance gauges, which consisted of a pointer that pivoted across a distance scale according to the angle at which the device was held. Pointing the apparatus at the base of the subject by looking through a sighting tube varied the angle, and the needle indicated the distance. By and large, however, the photographer's instinct, already called into use for ascertaining the correct exposure, was also adept at guessing a subject's distance, which he then set on the lens.

All of this – aperture and shutter speed adjustment, distance measurement and lens focusing – became second nature to professional photographers, who looked at the light, looked at the subject and made the settings almost without thinking.

These exposure and focusing basics applied equally to many of the small amateur cameras like the Vest Pocket Kodak, as well as larger professional models like the Goerz Anschütz. Using an amateur camera with roll film was then relatively easy. It was just a matter of loading the film, winding it until the figure one appeared in a red window on the back of the body, shooting the picture and winding it until the number two appeared, and so on until the end of the film. Professional cameras that used glass plates instead of film, however, presented even more complications.

The shutter would likely to have been a focal plane type that consisted of two blinds that ran across the back in front of the photographic plate or behind the lens. It had to be wound before it could be released, when

The No.3A Autographic Kodak Special, the first camera with a built-in rangefinder.

the first blind travelled across the back, followed by the second. Shutter speeds were controlled by a mixture of the gap between the blinds and the speed with which they moved. Each of the glass plates that the photographer needed to carry with him could be used for only one exposure at a time. Different models of camera took different sizes of plate. The Goerz Anschütz and equally popular Graflex Speed Graphic, both of which were used by professionals of the time, used plates of 4 × 5 inches. These were pre-loaded into holders protected from the light by a slat of wood called a dark slide. Once the shutter speed, lens aperture and focusing had been set, exposure involved inserting the plate holder, sliding out the dark slide, firing the shutter, replacing the dark slide and removing the plate holder, ready for storing away until its plate could later be removed in the dark and developed.

Using cameras like these in war zones was far from easy. Nevertheless, the soldiers took their cameras to war. Amateur photographer soldiers, despite the rules and regulations, went into battle with small roll

How a plate holder, with the plate protected by a dark slide, was inserted into the camera (shown with the dark slide partially removed). After the exposure, it was removed in a similar way.

For the photographer working in the field, a portable darkroom could be very useful, as advertised in 1916.

film cameras. Professionals travelled with their large format plate cameras. Some of these were designed for, or adapted by, the military. Most, however, were straightforward models, bought before the war began, and which were designed more for shooting in studios than in trenches. Developing and printing was often carried out in mobile or portable darkrooms.

A mobile darkroom used in France during the war.

The cameras that went to war

Vest Pocket Kodak

Two models of the Vest Pocket Kodak.

Made two years before the First World War broke out, then remarketed during wartime as The Soldier's Camera, this was a small folding model that amateur photographer soldiers kept in their tunic pockets and very often used illicitly to shoot pictures in places where the professionals couldn't easily reach. (See previous chapter for more information about this camera.)

Ensignette
Although the Vest Pocket Kodak was the camera that won fame for being small, easily carried and simple to use, it was predated by this English camera, made in 1909 by the Houghton company. It had all the conveniences of the Vest Pocket Kodak, and was actually easier to use, since the lens was fixed focus so didn't have to be adjusted for distances,

Two models of the Ensignette, one folded, the other ready for shooting.

the shutter had only a fixed speed and exposure was controlled by the use of just three apertures. There were three models of different sizes, the smallest folding to just $10 \times 5 \times 2$cm and extending on bellows supported by metal struts to a depth of 8.5cm for shooting. Launched in 1909, it immediately became extremely successful and popular for a new breed of snapshot photographer who demanded quality results coupled with simplicity of operation, and it is highly likely that many Ensignettes found their way into the pockets and kitbags of soldiers who went to war. The Ensignette was overshadowed, as was so often the case when Kodak launched a product, by the Vest Pocket Kodak in 1912, and after that its popularity waned.

Kodak No.1A Autographic Junior

It's probable that officers in the war were more likely to own cameras and less likely to be prosecuted for having them than was the case with the lower ranks. So while the enlisted men used small cameras, the better to keep them hidden, officers were likely to have used larger folding models, of which the No.1A Autographic Junior, launched in 1914, proved to be a popular choice. It took the form of so many folding cameras of the time, a flat box that measured $20 \times 9 \times 3$cm, from which a bed folded down to allow the lens to be pulled out along rails. Focus depended on where the lens was allowed to come to rest. With only two shutter speeds and a good range of apertures on the lens, the camera would have been capable of decent results in the right light. Its autographic feature allowed the photographer to write details of the picture taken onto the backing paper of special film, so that the words would be exposed onto the negative.

The popular Kodak No.1A Autographic Junior.

Kodak No.2 Brownie

The first Brownie was launched in 1900, but a year later, Kodak produced the more popular No.2 version. It was an archetypal box camera, which began a style that lasted for more than half a century. Indeed, many other box cameras not even made by Kodak became generically known as 'Box Brownies'. Unlike the folding cameras more favoured by the troops, this was a rigid box, which would have been impossible to hide in a tunic pocket. With the bare minimum of controls to worry about, the camera was very easy to use, though not as versatile as some better-specified models. For that reason it would have given poor results in less than perfect light. Nevertheless, as one of the most popular snapshot cameras of the era, it found its way into kitbags and was used covertly by enlisted troops as and when opportunities arose.

Kodak's No.2 Brownie, which popularised box cameras in general and also introduced 120 size film.

Goerz Anschütz

Although originally made as early as 1896, this was a camera that remained popular with press photographers and then professional army photographers throughout the war years. Even though it was used by the British, the camera was made in Berlin. It used glass plates and took the form of a folding camera in which the lens panel pulled out on bellows supported by metal struts from the part of the body that housed the plates and focal plane shutter. Setting a shutter speed involved two controls: one for the speed of the blinds, the other to set the gap between them. Three sizes of camera were made to take different size plates of 6×9cm, 9×12cm and 10×13cm. The last of these, more popularly known as 4×5 inches, was the size mostly used by professional military photographers.

The Goerz Anschütz, folded and unfolded.

ICA Minimum Palmos

The style of this camera was very similar to that of the Goerz Anschütz, with a lens pulling out from the back on bellows supported by struts. It was made from 1909 and it is pretty certain that a 9×12cm version was used by British professional photographers on the Western Front. As well as the 9×12cm size, the cameras were made to take 4.5×6cm, 6.5×9cm and 10×15cm size glass plates or sheets of cut film.

ICA's Minimum Palmos, folded and unfolded.

Graflex 1a

This was unusual among cameras in use during the war in that it was a single lens reflex, a style of camera that incorporated a mirror behind the lens to reflect its image onto a ground-glass viewing screen under a hood on top of the body. As the shutter release was pressed, the mirror flipped up and allowed light from the lens to then reach the film at the back of the camera. In this way the photographer could preview exactly what would appear on film before the picture was taken, as opposed to the use of the separate viewfinder found on other cameras of the time whose view never showed exactly the same scene taken in by the lens and so recorded on film or plate.

The lens panel was on bellows and ran on rails along a bed that folded up into the body. A knob on the side of the drop-down bed moved the lens panel back and forth for focusing, apertures were set on the lens and the shutter was a focal plane type set by controls on the back of the body. It was set with a combination of numbers, which referred to the speed of the blinds, and by the width of the slit between them. A small chart fixed to the back of the focusing hood explained how those combinations translated into conventional shutter speeds. The large viewfinder hood also folded down into the top of the body. Folded, the camera measured $25.5 \times 12.5 \times 15.5$cm. Unfolded, those measurements increased to $20.5 \times 25 \times 30$cm. It weighed 3.5 kilograms. So what it gained from the convenience of reflex viewing, it lost in its size, weight

Graflex 1a, a large and somewhat unwieldy single lens reflex, with a roll of its larger than usual 116 size roll film.

and consequential difficulty of use. The film was on a roll. It was called 116 and produced six pictures of 6.5 × 10.8cm. Spare rolls of film could be stored in compartments on either side of the body.

The Graflex 1a was also one of the few non-Kodak cameras to incorporate the autographic function, so details of a picture could be transcribed onto the film at the time of exposure, using a stylus clipped to the top of the body beside the focusing hood.

Richard Verascope

Stereo photography used twin-lens cameras to shoot two images of the same scene simultaneously. With the two lenses spaced apart by about the distance of human eyes, the resulting pictures, from very slightly different angles, were similar but not exactly the same. When the two pictures were inserted into a stereo viewer so that the left eye saw only the image shot by the camera's left lens, and the right eye saw only the picture from the right lens, then the brain combined the two into one stereoscopic, or three-dimensional, image that conveyed the impression of depth in exactly the way our eyes naturally see. Stereo cameras were particularly popular during the early part of the twentieth century when, during the war, they were used to record army life and also to produce souvenir images for the folks back home. The Richard Verascope, of which many models in different seizes were made from the 1890s onwards, was a typical French stereo model used for this purpose. It was a metal bodied camera, which took its twin pictures on cut film or glass plates. The cameras were more popular in France than in Britain.

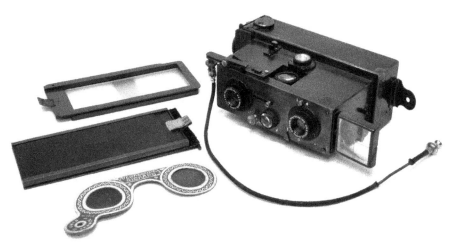

The French Richard Verascope with its stereo focusing screen, plate holder and stereoscopic viewing spectacles.

The importance of aerial photography

Before the First World War, the idea of aerial photography was treated with scepticism and as something of a novelty. Until then, reconnaissance was largely carried out by cavalry troops, infiltrating enemy lines and reporting back their findings. The earliest known manned flight was made in America when Wilbur and Orville Wright took to the air with the first powered heavier-than-air machine. That was in December 1903. In the following decade, aviation technology moved at a fast pace until, by the time of the outbreak of war, biplanes, with their double set of wings above and below the fuselage, abounded and began to be adopted by the military, first for general reconnaissance and then for aerial photography.

The French were the first to begin using cameras to photograph the German front from the air. By 1915, the British were following their example as an experimental group was formed to organise a unit for aerial photography and to develop a camera especially for use from aircraft. The group worked closely with the British Thornton Pickard company, who had for many years produced high-quality wooden plate cameras.

Thornton Pickard's first camera was the Type A. It had a wooden body, bound with brass in a design that tapered from the back where the 5 × 4-inch plates were held, to the lens at the front. It was used by simply

Aerial cameras used by the French air force during the First World War. The plate sizes and focal lengths of the lenses are marked on the chest they are standing on.

holding it over the side of the cockpit. The Type B camera that followed used the full-plate size of 6½ × 8½ inches and was suitable for lenses with longer focal lengths that made it easier to shoot detail on the ground from the height of the aircraft. Both of these cameras needed to be brought back inside the aircraft to change the plate between exposures, but the Type C camera that came next was fitted with a semi-automatic plate-changing device. This meant that it could be mounted vertically on the outside of the aircraft alongside the cockpit, with the shutter operated by the pilot by pulling a cord before automatically changing plates by pulling a lever on the top.

It was an awkward business, but because of the large format of the plates, the quality of the pictures was high, providing the photographer remembered to use a fast shutter speed to counteract the vibrations of the aircraft. Very often the pictures were shot in a sequence that allowed the final prints, after development, to be pieced together like a mosaic to show huge areas of the landscape below. Such mosaic-type maps were shot and examined before an attack to give troops on the ground advance warning of the enemy's strengths and weaknesses before battle commenced. Many thousands of these mosaic-maps were produced throughout the war, more than 19,000 aerial photographs being produced during the Battle of the Somme alone.

As the war progressed, and the value of using cameras in this way became more apparent, research and manufacture were stepped up and new types of camera were produced. Fixed to the sides of the aircraft, these were triggered remotely by the observer or even the pilot. Later, the old fashioned plate cameras were replaced by new models that used roll film. Lenses too became more sophisticated until it was possible to produced good-quality images from as high as 20,000 feet.

When historians talk of the First World War, they speak much of the war on the ground and the work of the artillery units. But without aerial photography, soldiers on the ground would have had far less information about whom and where to attack, or knowledge of what they might find when advancing on the enemy. In short, the part played by aerial photography was one of the most important weapons of the First World War.

The Doppel-Sport Pigeon Camera

Aeroplanes were the obvious choice from which to shoot aerial photographs of war. But if a slightly obscure German plan had worked out better, aircraft might have been replaced by pigeons.

Julius Neubronner was a German pharmacist and pigeon fancier who used homing pigeons to deliver prescriptions. When, one day, one of his pigeons stayed away for much longer than usual, he grew curious about where the bird had been. So, the next time the bird was released, Neubronner strapped a small camera to its chest to take pictures during

A panoramic swing-lens camera attached to a pigeon for aerial reconnaissance.

the flight. It led to Neubronner being granted a patent entitled *Method of and Means for Taking Photographs of Landscapes from Above.*

In the patent, Neubronner described a carrier pigeon equipped with a camera that used a pneumatically time-controlled shutter effecting exposure when the bird was over a required part of the landscape below. The frame to which the camera was attached was made of aluminium adapted to the shape of the bird and was attached to it by crossed leather bands. To this, the camera was attached by a spring.

Several types of camera were used, but the most popular was a panoramic type, using a swing-lens design, made popular by Kodak Panoram cameras at the end of the nineteenth and start of the twentieth centuries. In this type of camera, the lens, rather than pointing straight at the subject, pointed instead to one side. It was contained at the end of a cylinder with a slit at the opposing end, and the film was fed around a semicircular path. As the shutter was released, the lens swung in an arc while its image, projected through the slit, was built up gradually on the film in an extra-wide, panoramic format.

From 1909 to 1911, Neubronner took his birds, cameras and a mobile darkroom combined with a pigeon loft around various expositions in Germany, demonstrating his methods of taking aerial photographs and selling them as postcards. With the outbreak of war, the German military took an interest and attempts were made to use pigeons with cameras for aerial surveillance. Although some success was reported, the idea was eventually abandoned.

Life-saving cameras

A lot of stories were told during the First World War of soldiers whose lives were saved because various inanimate objects in tunic pockets and backpacks had obstructed bullets. Among the many metal obstacles that took bullets meant for their owners were cans of corned beef, pocket watches, hip flasks – and, of course, cameras. Letters from soldiers to the offices of Kodak in 1915 revealed two such incidents.

The first, sent to Kodak's London office, was from a British soldier. Here's what he had to say...

On 26 August I had some wonderful escapes. I was hit four times, and each time luck saved me. The first one I got in the pack, number two on the left elbow that put out the chap on my left, number three – the worst – went clean through a No.1 Folding Pocket Kodak that I had in my haversack, otherwise it would have gone through my hips. Number four stuck in a tin of bully beef.

The soldier who wrote the letter was later captured by the Germans and went on to escape, but he lost the camera...

I'm sorry I lost the small Kodak. The Germans took everything. It would have been a splendid souvenir.

The second letter was sent to Kodak's Berlin office, along with a picture of a camera with a bullet hole in its back and bellows...

The No.3 Folding Pocket Kodak that saved the life of one soldier.

The enclosed photograph of a No.3 Folding Pocket Kodak may be of interest to you. It was carried by an Austrian officer over his shoulder in a leather case. During a battle he received a shot which passed through the back of the camera, hit against the lens ring, passed through the bellows against the shutter and remained in the body of the Kodak. When he opened his camera, the bullet fell out. He says it undoubtedly saved his life, preventing what would otherwise have been a shot in the abdomen.

Movie cameras

By 1914, movie cameras, which had begun in the late nineteenth century and progressed in an episodic way with different mechanisms and various gauges of film, had largely settled down to a basic mechanical style that used 35mm film moved through the camera by the operator turning a crank on the side of the body at a steady and measured pace.

Like a still camera, a movie camera needed the operator to have knowledge of the relationships between shutter speeds, apertures and focusing. Unlike still cameras, the shutter speed was constant, measured not in fractions of a second like those in a still camera, but by the number of frames per second that the film was wound through the gate where the exposures were made. That wasn't as simple as it sounds. If the handle was turned too fast the projected image would show the action moving too slowly; turn the handle too slow and the projected image would move too fast. Trained cinematographers of the time developed an instinct for turning the crank at exactly the right number of rotations per second needed to produce the correct result. In this way exposure was controlled with the frames per second count at a constant speed, while adjusting lens apertures. Focus was carried out in the same way as with a still camera.

Many different, but similar, movie cameras of the time were used by cinematographers with the appropriate authority to move into action. Two cameras – one used by British forces, the other by the Americans – are worth considering in some detail.

Moy and Bastie

Ernest Moy was in charge of lighting at Her Majesty's Theatre in London when he met fellow electrical engineer Percy Bastie and, in 1895, they set up a company together, originally to produce electrical goods like fuses and switches. They went on to patent various ideas for movie cameras including one that accompanied Captain Robert Scott on his 1901–1904 expedition to the Antarctic. In 1909, the partners produced their most famous camera, and one that won them a place in cinematic history.

The Moy and Bastie camera was made in what was known as the upright style, meaning it was taller than it was wide or deep, and it was enormous, measuring $46 \times 40.5 \times 23$cm. The body was made of mahogany with metal fittings. Inside, it took two 400ft reels of 35mm film, which ran through the camera by means of a chain movement operated by the hand crank on the side. When it was launched, the camera cost £108, the equivalent of about £12,500 today. When the camera was mounted on its sturdy tripod, bringing it up to the height of its operator, it was even more enormous, making it and the person behind it an easy target for enemy snipers. Even so, it was used by official British cameramen with the armed forces during the First World War.

Two particular cameramen have gone down in history for the use of a Moy and Bastie camera. They were Lieutenant Geoffrey Mallins, a British film director, and fellow British cinematographer John McDowell. Together they were assigned to shoot movie footage on the Western Front. Because the camera was so large and cumbersome and because it made them easy targets for the enemy, it often proved impossible to shoot actual footage of soldiers climbing out of trenches in any form of close-up. For that reason, the cinematographers had to sometimes resort to shooting recreations of the events, though never in a way that changed the veracity of the real situations.

On their return to England, the film they shot was edited and turned into a feature film for cinema release. It was called *The Battle of the Somme*, and around 20 million tickets were sold to see it. More than any other film or still pictures from the various conflicts, it had a huge impact, which brought a new perception of the war to shocked audiences throughout the land, where many were ignorant of the real scale of death and destruction that was going on in Europe. John McDowell was later awarded the Military Cross for his courage under fire.

Moy and Bastie movie camera, popular among war cinematographers.

Akeley Camera

Carl Akeley was an American sculptor, biologist, conservationist, taxidermist, wildlife explorer and nature photographer. He was also the inventor of the Akeley Camera, a strangely designed model first seen in 1915. It had an unusual round, drum-shaped flat body that earned it the nickname of the Pancake.

What set the camera apart from its contemporaries was a revolutionary kind of shutter mechanism that allowed more light to reach the film, useful for Akeley's wildlife filming, much of which took place at dusk. The camera used two lenses, one for shooting the film, the other to act

The Akeley Camera, also known as the Pancake, in action.

as a viewfinder, and utilised an internal gyroscope that allowed the body and shooting lens to be tilted straight up. The camera took 35mm film in 400ft magazines that could be easily changed in as little as fifteen seconds. As well as wildlife filming, the camera was also used greatly by newsreel photographers.

Soon after America entered the First World War in 1917, Akeley offered to make his camera available to the American military's newly created photographic division. With so many military activities taking place at dusk, dawn and in other difficult lighting conditions, the camera's ability to shoot in low light was seen to be of prime importance. Test shots were made by Signal Corps cameraman Victor Fleming, who later in life would go on to become the well-known film director of *The Wizard of Oz* and *Gone with the Wind*.

The tests were positive and Akeley cameras were quickly adopted by the American Signal Corps to be used extensively on the Western Front. First used on the ground for documentary purposes, they were later also employed for aerial reconnaissance.

Kodak goes to war

Even though amateur photographers taking cameras into war zones was actively discouraged by the authorities, using a camera to document the war was something that Kodak was keen to encourage. In 1915, an issue of Kodak's magazine *Kodakery* ran an article headed 'The Kodak as a News Getter'. In it, readers were told…

> The war is establishing the Kodak amateur in a brand new field of usefulness. From a popular pastime, his Kodak turns to chronicling world events. From the romance of the summer wood it turns to the romance of war. And it is doing this work of war recording with graphic realism, absolute impartiality and splendid pictorial charm.

It's doubtful that British soldiers up to their necks in muck and bullets, as life in the trenches was popularly described at the time, would have been overly sympathetic to the expressions *romance of war*, or *splendid pictorial charm*. But this was 1915. *Kodakery* was published in Canada

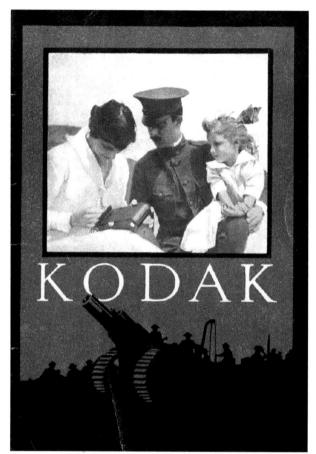

The cover of Kodak's annual equipment catalogue in 1918 reflected the part played by the company's cameras in the war.

and America, and although Canada was officially at war, being part of the British Empire, America was still neutral. Maybe the now unknown Kodak employee, sitting in an office on the other side of the Atlantic writing copy for the magazine, couldn't appreciate the horrors that were taking place in Europe. Nevertheless, the article continued by describing how professional photographers had used Kodak cameras in past conflicts such as the Balkan Wars, before continuing...

> Thousands of Kodaks are in the kits of soldiers at the front. Thousands more are in the hands of civilians within the war zone. And the shutters of all these are 'getting' the story of the greatest of all wars as only pictures can.

The article continued by postulating what it might have meant to history if there had been Kodak cameras in the time of the Caesars, Napoleon or the sailors who sailed with Christopher Columbus. Instead of a past wrapped in a veil of mystery, history would be flooded with light, it implied …

> All this will suggest to the wide-awake amateur a new era for his camera activities – an opening which is practically unlimited in its possibilities. Add to the pictorial and photographic quality of the picture a news value and the amateur becomes an important arm of the newspaper service, or a chronicler, possibly, of world events.

The article writer also pointed out that it was not strictly necessary to go to war to get news pictures, explaining that some of the most interesting 'war' pictures that had already been published were taken by Kodak travellers in times of peace, who were innocent of the fact that their subjects might soon become of both news and historic interest…

> Many Kodakers' landmarks the war has destroyed; but records of points of interest like Malines, Rheims, Brussels and Ostend are preserved in indestructible film. This fact alone would put the world under ever-lasting obligation to photography.

That 1915 issue of *Kodakery* magazine also included pictures taken by war photographers, which according to the article writer told their story 'with an intimacy and pitiless detail that is only possible to Kodak records'. These and other pictures were, the article concluded, 'some of the most interesting and intimate human documents ever published'.

Postcards

The first postcards were produced in Austria in 1869 as a way of reducing the time spent on writing a letter, addressing an envelope and the cost of posting it. The craze quickly spread through Europe. The earliest examples were little more than sheets of plain cardboard, but soon pictures were added, both artwork and photographs. By the time of the First World War, buying, sending and receiving postcards had reached its

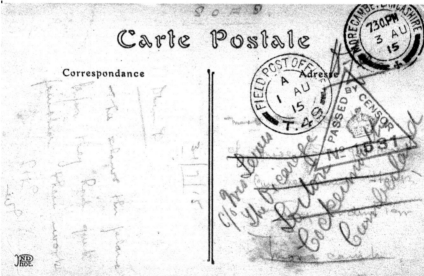

Front and back: a postcard sent home from France, and how it was passed by a censor before it left the country.

peak, as civilians and soldiers corresponded regularly from war zone to home and back again. The speed with which the cards could be delivered via army field post offices could be as little as two days.

Even soldiers in the trenches had opportunities to send cards, although the words they wrote on them were highly censored. Mostly they were confined to sending officially supplied cards pre-printed with terse messages such as 'I am well' or 'I have been wounded', to which they were not allowed to add anything more. However, the trade for postcards flourished, and in village shops behind the front lines soldiers could find commercially produced souvenirs of the war in the shape of individual cards showing photographs of damaged buildings or albums of similar cards designed to be torn out and posted.

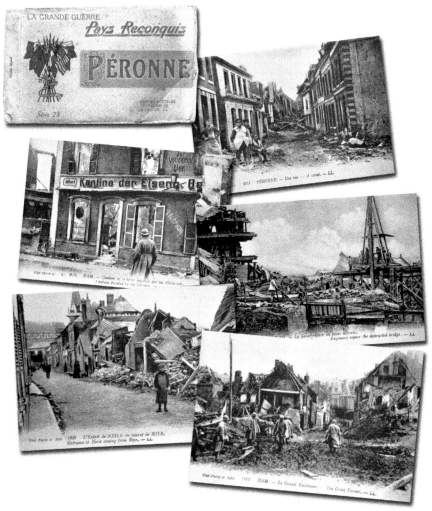

An album and some of the postcards it contained, showing the ruins of Péronne, a town very close to the Somme, where some of the fiercest battles of the war were fought in 1916.

Postcards from the town of Péronne in northern France stand as an example of the kind of album produced at this time. Today Péronne is a thriving and beautiful little town, known for its thirteenth-century castle and a museum dedicated to the history of the First World War. During that war, however, the town stood close to where the 1916 plus the first and second 1918 battles of the Somme took place, when more than 3 million men fought and 1 million were wounded or killed, making it one of the bloodiest battles in human history. From this came an album titled *La Grande Guerre: Pays Reconquis* (*The Great War: Reconquered Country*). It contained eighteen postcards, each with a picture on the front and the usual place to write an address and message on the back. All the cards were detachable so that each might have been removed, written on and posted, and every card illustrated an image of what remained of the town in total ruins.

By contrast, postcards back home designed for civilians to send to their loved ones overseas were more light-hearted. One such, for example, showed a photograph of a young lady writing a letter with an inset picture of a soldier reading it. Headed with the words 'Thoughts of you', the card also contained a sentimental poem...

When Duty's call came loud and clear, how proud I was to see,
My dearest one go like a man, to fight for liberty.
And when at last our Victory's won and Peace once more shall reign,
No heart will be more glad than mine, to have you back again.

Partly because photography during the First World War was so heavily censored, its true horrors were not readily appreciated by those back home. As a result, the triviality of some of the civilian postcards of this era bore a sharp contrast to the harshness and horror of the war that inspired them. Consider, for example, one postcard that showed a First World War tank rumbling over a rocky landscape, and into which the card designer had inserted a flap that opened to reveal a concertina-folded strip of typical peacetime seaside pictures. Across the top the words read 'A tank full of memories from Brighton'. Such was the way 'Brighton' was printed on the card, it was clear that it had been designed to be reprinted with the name of any other suitable seaside resort inserted.

Postcards available at home for sending to troops overseas were rather more sentimental than those being sent home by soldiers at war.

The photographs of ruined towns that were shown on postcards overseas might at first seem inappropriate on a medium more often associated with sending happy messages. But at least they showed the reality of the war, rather than the misguided romance of war that many experienced at home.

Business as usual

Reading how some civilian commentators and photographic company advertisements reported on, and referred to, the war, it's difficult to know whether they were acting as purveyors of propaganda, being plainly naïve, or just taking advantage of the climate to sell more products.

The *British Journal Photographic Almanac* was published annually to review the latest equipment and processes but because its deadlines were anything up to a year in advance of publication, it was 1915 before the first references to war began to appear, when Editor George E. Brown wrote...

As was to be expected, the present disastrous European War has had a considerable influence upon the extent to which firms in the photographic trade have taken advantage of the wide advertising powers of the *Almanac*. Channels of trade have been interrupted and supplies of raw materials disturbed. Yet the effect is really less than might have been anticipated.

The following year, Mr Brown reported that the previous twelve months had been a time of much embarrassment to those engaged in the manufacture of photographic materials and apparatus...

Lack of raw materials, deficiencies in transport and shortage of labour are difficulties which makers have and still have to experience and, therefore, it is a matter for congratulation that the disturbance of conditions so far as concerns the production of plates and papers has been as small as it has. So far, as concerns apparatus, there are few factories which have not been engaged to the utmost in the manufacture of goods for the national services of a kind appropriate to their facilities.

An advertisement in 1915 for a company called Hood and Co. Ltd., who were engravers and printers, began by declaring that the chief business of the country now should be fighting and that the numbers and efficiency of our soldiers are vastly more important than maintenance 'as usual' of British factories. Having got that off their chest, they went on to point out...

You can do at least two things which open up new channels of profit. Can you imagine any happier gift to our soldiers in the trenches than portraits or groups of the dear ones at home? The other way, and a brilliantly profitable one, is to make the most of every incident

How advertisements for one photographic company changed from peacetime to the war years.

JOHNSON'S CHEMICALS

BRITISH MADE

JOHNSON'S CHEMICALS

for OVERSEAS

JOHNSON'S CHEMICALS

For HOME and EXPORT

As the war progressed, patriotic pictures graced the adverts for Johnson's photographic chemicals, as advertised in 1916, 1917, 1918 and 1919.

bearing in the least on military or naval matters by issuing Hood ONE-DAY post cards.

The previous year, the Hood advertisement had been illustrated with a picture of a young lady looking into a lily pond. In 1915, that was replaced by a picture of the battleship *Neptune*. The following year, a Zeppelin airship graced the company's advertisement. Despite the fact that the Germans were using them for bombing raids over Britain, the caption was keen to tell readers that the illustration was from a publication called *East Coast Raids Memorial*, published by Hood, available by post for 11d (approximately 5p).

By 1917, illustrated by a portrait of King George V, available post-free for 1s 3d (approximately 6p), the Hood advertisement greeted its readers 'whether in studio or trench' by telling them...

It is certain that anything which ministers to the happiness and convenience of either of the troops or their relatives deserves to be profitable; and this is why many photographers have experienced astonishingly good times lately.

During the war, photographic advertisements soon started to show patriotic images. In 1916, an advert for Johnson's photographic chemicals was illustrated, not by the usual bottles of liquid or packets of powder, but with a full colour picture of a battleship overlaid with a Royal Navy White Ensign flag. It was followed in subsequent years with pictures of troops in battle, a biplane flying over a sea full of battleships and, as the war ended, ships steaming up the Thames towards Tower Bridge standing against a sunset.

Effects on the photo trade

The outbreak of war did little initially to affect the profits of photographic companies. In its annual report for the year ended 31 December 1915, Kodak showed a profit of £3,245,660, the largest in the history of the company. As the war progressed, matters changed dramatically.

Foreign companies who had previously enjoyed business in Britain didn't do so well. Soon after Britain became involved in the First World

War, an Act of Parliament, known as the Trading with the Enemy Act of 1914, came into force, making it an offence to conduct business with any person of 'enemy character'. The Board of Trade then went on to order the discontinuance of businesses for a list of companies of enemy nationality. Along with companies concerned with everything from the sale of aluminium foil to importers of cutlery, the list included photographic and optical firms such as Emil Busch, C.P. Goerz, Felix Schoeller and A. Tospann.

The misfortune of some enemy companies soon became the fortune of their British counterparts. In 1917, The City Sale and Exchange, a London-based dealership calling themselves the leading specialists in everything photographic, announced that under the Trading with the Enemy Act and by arrangement with the Board of Trade…

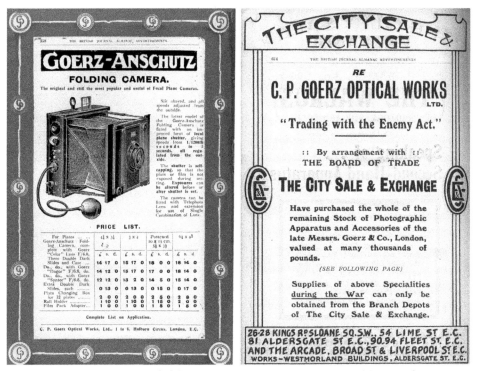

The German company of C.P. Goerz was one of the photographic manufacturers no longer welcome to advertise their products in Britain after 1914, while British photographic dealers like City Sale and Exchange profited from buying up German stock from Goerz and selling it to British photographers.

The City Sale and Exchange have purchased the remaining stock of photographic apparatus and accessories of the late Messrs Goerz & Co, London, valued at many thousands of pounds. Supplies of the specialities, during the war, can only be obtained from the branch depots of the City Sale and Exchange.

The company's advertisements went on to list the Goerz Anschütz cameras of the time that were used by many British military photographers, together with Tenax cameras, lenses, enlargers, telescopes and all kinds of photographic accessories. The goods were available at pre-war prices and it was made clear that supplies were limited. Catalogues were available on application.

The longer the duration of the war, the more manufacturers suffered. J. Lizars, the manufacturer of Challenge cameras, advertised as all-British instruments of quality, announced in 1917 that the manufacture of 'an excellent series of new cameras of most beautiful design is delayed for the duration of the war'. Ross Ltd., who made lenses and cameras, announced that the fulfilment of orders could not be guaranteed until after the war, although customers were still urged to send for catalogues with information of what they could buy as soon as it was available. Newman and Guardia, manufacturers of high-class photographic apparatus, reminded customers that, by the fourth year of the war, the most difficult problem facing all manufacturers was shortage of material and labour for private work, while adding...

Our waiting list grows apace, and interested purchasers are urged to send in their orders to ensure earliest deliveries with orders completed in strict rotation.

Kodak at this time was keen to emphasise that its usual lists of photographic apparatus obtainable in all parts of the world would not be of much practical service, although...

The lines which are out of stock in one country are not necessarily those which are out of stock in another. In some cases, but not in others, the particular lines which are out of stock one month may happen to be in stock the next month.

Robert Ballantine, an optician and photographic dealer in Glasgow, summed up the situation perfectly, while blowing his own trumpet to some extent with a recommendation to his customers in this way...

All factories of importance are presently engaged on work of national interest, consequently the supplies of new apparatus have practically come to a standstill. The result of this has been a substantial increase in the price of second-hand outfits, and unfortunately it has been the means of a considerable quantity of old, unreliable and obsolete material being thrown on the market, which but for the prevailing circumstances would never have been considered worthy of being again utilised for photographic work.

It is owing to this VERY UNCERTAIN QUALITY that some SAFEGUARD is necessary, and the most effective way to combat the evil is to place your confidence in one who has been before the photographic public for thirty years. IT IS TO YOUR ADVANTAGE AT ALL TIMES, AND MORE PARTICULARLY NOW, TO SELECT A DEALER WHO WILL PERSONALLY LOOK AFTER YOUR INTERESTS IN THE CHOICE OF YOUR APPARATUS. I subject all outfits to a MOST SEARCHING AND CRITICAL EXAMINATION AND TEST, so that my clients escape the unpleasant experience of finding upon receipt of goods some fault which necessitates the return of the article. Photographers generally will appreciate the value of SUCH ASSURANCE AND THOROUGH METHODS, and at the same time find that my prices compare favourably with those of any other established house.

After the war

The end of the First Word War was signalled by the German surrender on 11 November 1918, and the war formally ended with the signing of the Treaty of Versailles on 28 June 1919. By then, the photographic industry was beginning to get itself together again. Even so, manufacturers would be hampered by the lack of materials and the labour necessary to build the equipment for a few years more.

The Ross Optical Works in London announced that manufacture of lenses had been resumed and that every effort would be made to give prompt delivery of all orders, adding...

In the event of any unavoidable delay under the still abnormal conditions, we claim the kind indulgence of our customers.

The Raines Service, a company based in London and involved with all forms of developing, printing and mounting of photographs, was employed throughout the war by the British, Colonial and Allied governments to produce exhibitions of war photographs in colour for propaganda purposes. In all, Raines produced twenty-seven exhibitions of naval and military photographs, as well as making on average 11,000 smaller propaganda enlargements. By the end of the war, the company's output was three times as much as it had been in 1914, as it announced...

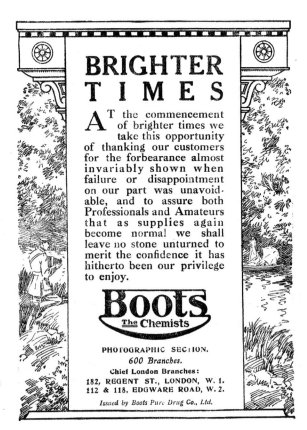

As the war ends, Boots the Chemist reports brighter times ahead.

At the earliest possible moment, consistent with Government requirements, we shall place this new and greatly improved Raines Service at the disposal of the world's photographers. Enemy subjects barred.

Camera and scientific instrument makers Newman and Guardia announced that they were already indulging in pleasurable anticipation of the resumption of normal conditions...

> Whatever the immediate future has in store, we have no hesitation in inviting intending purchasers to pass us their orders for completion in strict rotation, as the various models reach us from our factory. Our works have been largely extended and entirely re-equipped with the latest machinery.

The problems of peace were outlined by James A. Sinclair and Co. Ltd., makers of plate, reflex and movie cameras...

> During the war period our works have been under Government control and, as a consequence, the output of our main specialities has had to cease, or at least such of them as have required metal workers for their production. It may take some years before we are in a position to supply all our pre-war lines. We shall, however, hope to shortly be in a position to manufacture the N.S. Kinema Camera, Patent Reflex Camera and Centum Camera.

Slowly but surely, the photographic trade began to rebuild itself, and in the years that followed, before the outbreak of the Second World War, many new and important innovations in camera design made their debuts.

Chapter 6

Focus On: The Hythe Mark III Machine Gun Camera

With the outbreak of the First World War, Britain's air force began to develop into an organised unit within the country's fighting forces, and it became apparent that some method was required to quickly train airmen in the use of a machine gun mounted on an aeroplane. This required a method whereby a man could judge the distance from a moving base to a moving target, to align the gun on the object, to fire and hit that target, all with the minimum of conscious effort.

Obviously, the kind of training given to land units couldn't work in the air. On land, with a fixed base for the gun and a fixed target, a definite record could be made of marksmanship. In the air, with the positions of the gunner and his target constantly on the move, and with the light continually changing, it was a different matter. Also, unlike target practice on the ground, live ammunition could not be used, for fear of actually shooting down an aeroplane. Photography, already playing its role in air reconnaissance, was called in to solve the problem. The result was this unusual gun camera.

Background to the gun

In 1910, American inventor Samuel McLean sold his mechanical patent rights to the Automatic Arms Company of Buffalo. Among these rights was the design for a machine gun, but one that was so complex and full of largely unnecessary gadgets, that the arms company decided it wasn't worth manufacturing in its suggested form. So they turned to a US Army colonel, who was also an accomplished engineer, asking him to come up with a new design that, while based on McLean's original operating system, would be a lot simpler to build and use. The colonel's name was Isaac Newton Lewis, and the weapon he designed came to be called the Lewis gun.

Straight away, the visionary Colonel Lewis saw his gun as the ideal weapon for air-to-air combat and to prove the point, he set up a demonstration for the press. On 7 June 1912, Captain Charles DeForest Chandler, a commander in the US Army Air Service, took to the air in a Wright Type B aeroplane, armed with a Lewis gun, and became the first man in history to fire a machine gun in flight. The press thought it was a great idea, and pictures of the event went round the world. The American Army Ordnance Board thought otherwise. They tested the gun, found it wanting and decided not to adopt it. Disillusioned, Colonel Lewis retired from the army and set sail for Europe. In January 1913, he arrived in Belgium, where he had much more success in persuading that country's army to adopt his machine gun for their use. Within a short while, the Lewis gun was being manufactured at Liege to use British 0.303-inch calibre ammunition. Shortly afterwards, the Birmingham Small Arms Company in Britain obtained a licence to manufacture the weapon.

With the outbreak of the First World War, the Lewis gun became formerly adopted as the standard issue British Army machine gun. By 1916, approximately 50,000 had been produced, and the gun had earned a nickname from the German troops who came up against it. They called it the Belgian Rattlesnake. Regarded as the best and most reliable machine gun of its time, the Lewis gun was soon adapted by the Royal Navy for use at sea as an anti-aircraft weapon. And it found a home at last in the air where, used in the slipstream of an aeroplane or airship, it could be stripped of its barrel cooling jacket, making it even lighter and easier to use. It was also used mounted on tanks and even motorcycles.

The Lewis gun, which became the inspiration for a camera to train pilots in air-to-air combat.

Background to the camera

The British camera manufacturing company Thornton Pickard was founded in 1888 by Edgar Pickard and John Thornton, who had met the previous year at the Royal Jubilee Exhibition in Manchester, where Thornton was exhibiting his first camera. He had also been designing cameras and shutters with his business partner Reginald Nixon under the name of the Thornton Manufacturing Company. Even so, Thornton was by no means a rich man, and money in the business was tight. Pickard, on the other hand, came from a wealthy family, made rich by a wholesale grocery and a jam-making business in Mansfield. Hearing that Thornton needed cash to continue patenting his various ideas, Pickard raised capital from his father, bought out Nixon and, together with Thornton, started the new company, primarily to sell camera shutters. Three years later, they moved to purpose-built premises where they established a reputation for making high-quality wooden cameras.

It was not an easy partnership. The two men, coming from very different backgrounds, often failed to see eye to eye about business practices. In January 1897, the company became limited, and Thornton's patents became the property of the shareholders, most of whom were members of the Pickard family. When Pickard died a few months later, from peritonitis due to a perforated ulcer, it left his family in effective control of the company and his brother George was voted in as the new co-managing director to Thornton. Overworked and worried that his new partner was going to ruin the business, Thornton fell ill and then resigned, following which he was made to sever all connections with the business, the Pickard family taking out a court injunction to prevent him making cameras in Britain. Eventually, totally disillusioned, Thornton left for America, where he patented a three-colour cine film, which Eastman Kodak used under licence.

Meanwhile in England, the Thornton Pickard company carried on without him and continued to make a well-respected series of plate cameras. Despite this, however, the company began to go into decline in the years leading up to the First World War and, to survive, turned to government work, making aerial cameras throughout the war years. Now into the story comes the Royal Flying Corps, which had been formed in 1912. To that organisation fell the task of designing a sight recording camera. Two models were quickly built, but used only on a temporary basis while experiments were carried out on a more complete instrument that would take the place of a real gun. Its inventor was Major David Gedes, Commanding Officer of the Royal Flying Corps Gunnery School at Hythe in Kent.

With the Lewis gun so popular with the armed forces at the time, it became the natural choice of model for the camera, and with Thornton Pickard now heavily involved in government work, that was the company chosen to build it. The result, launched in 1915 and a million miles away from the kind of cameras more usually associated with Thornton Pickard, was the Mark III Hythe Camera – Mark III because it was the third version after the first two temporary models, Hythe because that's where it was designed and built.

The Mark III Hythe Camera with its accessory gun sights added.

The camera's design

The prime object of the camera gun was to make the gunner an efficient marksman. So the design involved a camera that looked like, and was used in a similar way to, a machine gun. The difference was that instead of shooting bullets, it shot pictures. When developed this indicated how accurate the gunner had been in lining up his target. But secondary to that was the fact that it would also train the airman to correctly

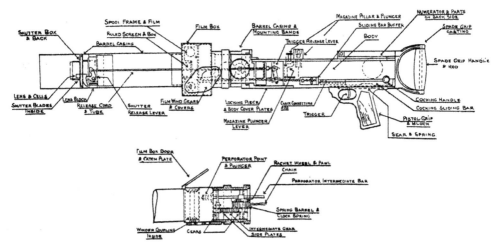

Schematic drawing of the gun camera, showing its internal workings.

handle the real weapon. This meant that a means had to be introduced to completely replicate the mechanical action of the gun as well as the aiming. Without that, the airman was likely to concentrate his attention on taking successful photographs rather than efficient manipulation of the weapon.

As new details about aerial combat were considered, more refinements were added to the camera until, in the end, it became an almost exact replica of the real thing, identical in size, shape and weight to the Lewis gun, right down to the fact that the design even incorporated the barrel cooling jacket, necessary for use of the gun, but totally superfluous on the camera.

The device was a monster, more than a metre long although the camera itself only took up around 40cm at the front. That took the form of a box containing a film carrier, into which the film was loaded. A screen was positioned in front of the film, which, depending on its type, recorded markings on the film either as a series of ruled lines dividing the screen into squares or as a series of concentric circles. The gun's barrel, in front of the film box, housed a 300mm f/8 lens. Behind that lay a three-leaf shutter with a single speed of around 1/150 second.

To the rear of the film box came the body of the gun, terminating in a large handle grip. In front of it, on top of the body, the film frame counter

The film carrier into which film was loaded.

The film box with the film carrier inserted.

was adjusted by a knob under the body and read through an aperture in the metal bodywork on the top. Beneath the body a pistol grip housed the trigger mechanism that fired the shutter, by means of a wire cable running from the trigger at the back of the body all the way to the shutter at the front.

On the side of the gun camera, a sliding bolt was connected internally by a chain to a brass barrel around which it was wound once. A spindle ran through the centre of the barrel with a ratchet on one end. This was arranged so that, as the bolt was slid back, the spindle revolved with the barrel, but as the bolt was returned, the spindle remained stationary. The spindle was also geared to a slotted gear wheel in the film box, which connected to another on the film's take-up spool. In this way, sliding back the bolt wound the film one frame. That brass barrel was also connected to a mechanism that, as it revolved, tensioned the shutter and, as the trigger was pulled, a spring dragged the barrel back to its original position.

Sliding the bolt also served one other purpose. As it was slid all the way back, it connected with a plate on which a ratchet engaged with a wheel with numbers around its edge. These were the numbers that could be seen beneath the aperture in the top of the camera body. Each time the bolt was slid back, the wheel turned and the number increased by one, which had the effect of counting the frames of film. A small spring moved the plate back to its original position as the shutter trigger was pulled. Gun sights, usually found on the top of the body and barrel, were

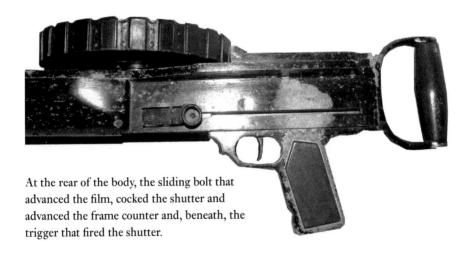

At the rear of the body, the sliding bolt that advanced the film, cocked the shutter and advanced the frame counter and, beneath, the trigger that fired the shutter.

not supplied with the camera, but real gun sights were obtainable for the purpose from the manufacturers.

The camera took 6×4.5cm negatives on roll film, and special 50 exposure rolls were available on application to Thornton Pickard soon after the camera's launch. The outfit, as sold by Thornton Pickard, included the lens, cartridge magazine, ruled screen in metal frame, roll film spool holder, shutter opening rod, mounting bands and pivot, all complete in a baize-lined, stained wood storage case with carrying handle.

The camera in action

Before loading the camera, the sights had to be adjusted, and this was a two-man operation. With the camera mounted on a tripod, it began with opening the shutter by means of a thin rod inserted into a small hole at the front of the barrel casing where it was gently pressed down. Next,

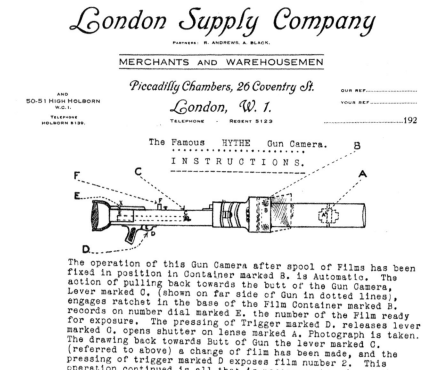

Instructions for use of the camera, as supplied by the London Supply Company.

the film carrier was withdrawn and replaced with a small prism mirror, supplied with the camera. With the shutter open, the ruled screen at the film plane was reflected in the mirror. Now, as one man looked through the sights on the top of the camera and positioned them on an object around 200 metres away, the second man looked at the image on the screen reflected in the mirror. If the sights were set correctly, the point where the screen's cross lines met should have been the exact point at which the sights were aimed. The screen could be moved backwards and forwards in a groove to adjust the sighting. With the sights set, the mirror was removed and the film carrier, now loaded with film, was inserted in its place.

To use the camera, the bolt on the side of the body was first pulled back to initially wind the film and then tension the shutter. Care had to be taken to pull the bolt all the way back; otherwise the film might be

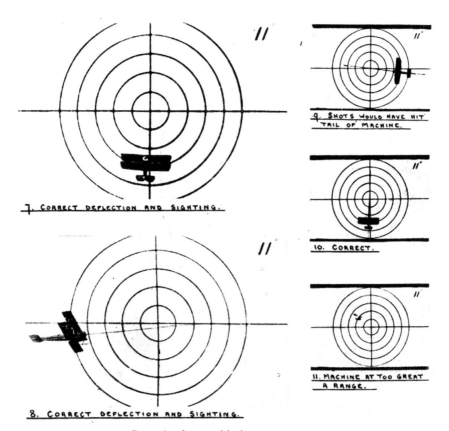

Records of tests with the gun camera.

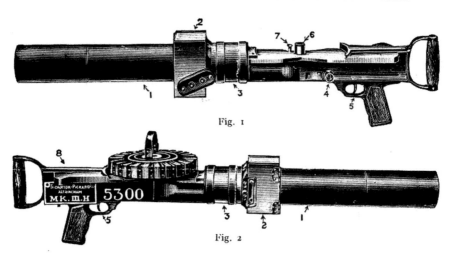

Mk. III Hythe Camera

Fig. 1

Fig. 2

In the barrel casing (1) is mounted the shutter and lens which focusses the image on to the sensitive film in the removable spool holder in the film box (2), interposing the light from the lens and in contact with the film is a ruled glass screen marking off the exposed area into circles of predetermined diameters so that the value and effectiveness of the aim may be recorded.

Behind the film box is the mechanism barrel and mounting bands, the hinged clips of the gun mounting are fastened around the bands, and inside the barrel is the mechanism connected to the cocking handle and to the film spool frame for changing the film after each exposure. No. 6 (Fig. 1) shows the magazine pillar and adjacent (No. 7) is the magazine plunger, which is depressed each time the cartridge magazine is placed in position. This operates a perforating device, making a hole in the sensitive film each time the magazine is placed in position. No. 4 (Fig. 1) is the cocking handle, which must be drawn along the slide to the set position previous to making each exposure, this movement bringing an unexposed length of film into place. No. 5 is the trigger for releasing the cocking slide actuated by a spring drum in the mechanism barrel. This slide before coming to the rest position strikes a trip lever which operates the shutter of the lens and makes the exposure on the film. No. 8 is the numerator aperture wherein is indicated the number of exposures made. In the improved 1922 model 50 exposures may be made without reloading.

The course of training involved by the use of this Camera " Gun " inculcates systematic subconscious action in manipulation, rapid judgment, and speedy decision with accurate marksmanship.

SPECIFICATION.

GUN CAMERA, complete as illustration, with Lens, Cartridge Magazine, Ruled Screen in metal frame, Roll Film Spool Holder, Shutter opening rod, Mounting bands and pivot. Complete in baize lined, stained wood, storage case, with carrying handle.

PRICE, complete as specification, £60.

Special 50 exposure films for above quoted on application.

How Thornton Pickard advertised the gun camera.

wound without the shutter being set for action. The trigger beneath the body was then pulled to trip the shutter and take the picture.

On the top of the body, between the rear handle and the film box, there was a fake magazine, which, on the real thing, would have housed bullets. This also served a useful purpose in the gunnery training. As the magazine was removed and replaced on the camera, it pushed down on a button that connected with a device to perforate a small hole in the film. This proved that the gunner had not only aimed and fired the gun correctly, but that he had also changed the magazine at the appropriate time, in the way he would have to if operating the real thing. In the words of Thornton Pickard literature of the time...

The course of training involved by the use of this Camera Gun inculcates systematic subconscious action in manipulation, rapid judgement and speedy decision with accurate marksmanship.

Once developed, the images on the film indicated how accurate the airman had been in aiming the camera and, if it had been a real gun, how likely it would have been that he had shot down an enemy aircraft.

Chapter 7

The Years Between the Wars

T he years between the end of the First World War in 1918 and the start of the Second World War in 1939 saw huge strides in the advancement of camera design. Projects that had been put on hold when war broke out were resurrected; photographic technology that had been developed and driven by the needs of war crossed over into civilian life; and totally new concepts were pioneered by photographic manufacturers whose names would become legend. Although large format plate cameras remained in popular use, especially in the professional world, a definite shift began towards smaller cameras that used rolls of film in place of the rigid plates. In the space of little more than twenty years, three iconic camera styles emerged from three different manufacturers, each of which went on to influence the designs of cameras worldwide, and all of which played important roles in the conflicts to come.

The first 35mm camera

Thirty-five millimetre film, originally made for use in movie cameras, came to still cameras in 1925 with the creation of one of photography's most iconic marques: the Leica. There had been cameras before that used 35mm film, but the Leica proved to be the camera in which its use was truly viable and it eventually became the most popular film size of all time, used by professional and amateur photographers alike. But it didn't start out that way.

Development of the camera that became the Leica began before the First World War in 1911, when Oskar Barnack joined E. Leitz, a family-run German optical company at Wetzlar in Germany, to take up the role of Director of Research. One of his first projects was to work on a high-quality movie camera. Such cameras in these early years were already taking 35mm film as their standard gauge, but the emulsion speeds of the films were unreliable and accurate metering was difficult. So Barnack turned to finding a way to test small batches of film, other than going to the expense of running it through a movie camera. In 1913 he designed and built a small piece of equipment for that purpose, but it soon occurred to him that what he had actually built was not so much a piece of film testing equipment, but something more like a miniature camera. A 35mm movie camera frame size measured 18 × 24mm, and the film ran vertically through the camera, but Barnack ran film through his prototype camera horizontally, doubling up on one of the dimensions of the frame. So was born the 24 × 36mm negative size that became the standard for 35mm still photography. It was clear to Barnack that this was an idea worth developing further, but then the First World War broke out and the project was put on hold.

With the end of the war, Barnack returned to his idea of producing a miniature camera, persuading Ernst Leitz, the head of the optical

The protoype built by Oscar Barnack that led to the first Leica.

company, to have thirty-one cameras handmade to test the market for his new type of camera. Reaction from scientists and photographers alike was sceptical, but Ernst Leitz decided to take the risk, despite the fact that his company had never before made a still camera for the general public. The name was derived from LEItz CAmera, and the first model was launched at the Leipzig Spring Fair in 1925.

Initially, such a small camera, producing such a tiny negative, was treated with suspicion. The following year, the *British Journal Photographic Almanac*, reviewing an early model of the camera, referred to it as the Leica Cine Film Camera, understandable in the light of the fact that 35mm had not before been seriously considered as a still camera format. Here's what the *Almanac* had to say...

Quite an innovation in pocket cameras is one just issued by the well-known firm of Leitz, designed to take about five feet of ordinary standard perforated cinematographe film, which is mounted in a special spool, allowing of daylight loading and unloading. Thirty-six exposures may be made without recharging the camera. The latter of high-class metal construction, measures about 5¼ × 2¾ × 1¾ inches and is fitted with a Leitz Elmax lens of 2 inches focal length and

The Leica I was the first truly viable 35mm camera.

f/3.5 aperture, arranged on a focusing mount. In design and workmanship, the camera is of the highest description.

In the years ahead, improvements were made to the original model as 35mm film became more accepted as a viable film size that was soon adopted by other camera makers. Cameras not just from Leica but from other makers, notably Zeiss Ikon, went on to play important roles in war photography during the coming Second World War and on into the Korean War. The 35mm format became the world's most popular film size, remaining so right up until the dawn of digital photography.

The first compact twin lens reflex

There was nothing new about the twin lens reflex (TLR) design, which went right back to the earliest plate cameras. Such cameras featured two lenses, one usually mounted above the other. The lower lens recorded its image on glass plates in the early days; the upper lens reflected its image, via a 45-degree mirror, up to a large ground-glass viewing screen on the top of the body. Early plate cameras of this design were bulky and best used on a tripod. The innovation that came about between the wars was taking the basic concept of the TLR, adapting it for roll film and reducing it to a smaller size that could be easily handheld for shooting. The company that produced this new take on an old design was Franke and Heidecke at Braunschweig in Germany.

The Franke and Heidecke company was formed in 1920, and its first camera was a stereo model with three lenses. The two outer lenses shot the stereo pair of pictures; the lens in the centre reflected its image to a ground-glass focusing screen on top of the body. It was called the Heidoscop. In 1926, a new version of the camera was made. The style was similar in that it used three lenses – two for shooting, one for view finding – but the difference was this camera was made to take roll film. Keeping part of the original name, but adding the 'roll' aspect, the new camera became the Rolleidoscop. From there, it was but a short step to take the basic design of the Rolleidoscop, turn the camera on its end, remove one lens and place the viewing screen on the top end of the body. Once again the name became a hybrid of former names, together with the

The Heidoscop stereo camera that led to the Rolleiflex.

reflex aspect of the design. Introduced in 1928, the camera was called the Rolleiflex. It was an immediate success.

The original Rolleiflex adopted the upright box shape that would become synonymous with TLR design. The shooting lens was a 75mm f/4.5 Tessar, and the shutter was speeded 1-1/300 second. It originally took six pictures, each one 6 × 6cm, on 117 size roll film, but later many cameras were converted to take twelve exposures of the same size on 120 roll film, a size that became standard for the vast majority of TLRs in the years ahead.

Film advance was by a knob with exposure numbers on the film's backing paper viewed through a red window on the back of the body. A second knob on the lower part of one side of the body was turned to move

The original Rolleiflex, the first small format twin lens reflex.

a panel, containing both lenses, back and forth for focusing. The ground-glass screen was found under a hood that flipped up from the top of the body and which incorporated a magnifier for accurate focusing. When the image on the screen was sharp, so too was the image on film.

Thanks to the success of the original Rolleiflex, the Franke and Heidecke company was able to expand, take on more staff and build new factories to cope with demand. Heidecke wasn't a man to rest on his laurels, however, and by 1931 he revolutionised the TLR design again and made the cameras even smaller. The result was the Baby Rolleiflex, similar to the original design, but made to take twelve exposures 4 × 4cm on 127 film.

In the years that followed, the company produced a new stripped-down and less expensive version of the Rolleiflex and called it the Rolleicord, while continuing to produce new models of the Rolleiflex, each with improved features that made it easy to use. Its name became synonymous with both manufacture of the cameras and the quality of the photographs they produced.

The basic designs of the Rolleiflex and Rolleicord went on to become templates for a vast number of similarly designed TLR cameras, made by a great many manufacturers all around the world. During the Second World War, TLRs began to replace the larger plate cameras until then used almost exclusively by professional photographers.

The first 35mm single lens reflex

What set the single lens reflex (SLR) apart from other cameras was the way its lens reflected an image via a mirror up to the viewfinder. In this way the photographer saw in advance exactly what would appear on film right up until the moment of exposure when the mirror flipped aside to allow the lens's light to reach the film. Like the TLR, the SLR design existed back in the days of plate cameras. The important innovation that eventually made the SLR probably the most popular camera type of all time was when one was made to take 35mm film.

The Ihagee company was established at Dresden in Germany in 1912. In 1933, Ihagee set out to make a smaller, more compact SLR, which took 127 size roll film. It was called the Exakta. That was the camera that

Exakta B, a roll film predecessor of the first 35mm single lens reflex.

paved the way for the first 35mm SLR in 1936. That one was called the Kine Exakta. Like its 127 film predecessor, the new camera's unusually shaped body tapered away on each side of the lens, making a kind of blunt pyramid shape, with the shutter release on the front beside the lens, rather than in its usual position on the top of the body. The instruction book was keen to point out that the camera was 'in good repute because of its manysidedness', a rather convoluted way of saying it was extremely versatile.

The lens reflected its image up to a small viewfinder screen under a hood on the top of the body, made to be used by looking down into the camera held at waist height. A magnifier could be flipped up from inside the hood to enlarge the viewfinder image for fine focusing. A range of standard, wide-angle and telephoto interchangeable lenses was available with bayonet mounts, along with accessories like extension tubes, bellows, microscope adapter and lens hoods. Shutter speeds from 1/1000

The Kine Exakta was the first singe lens reflex made for 35mm film.

to 1/25 second were set on a conventional shutter speed dial. Then the dial's 'B' setting, used in conjunction with a delayed-action knob at the opposite end of the top plate, offered extra slow speeds from 1/10 second down to a full twelve seconds.

The camera took conventional 35mm film in cassettes that gave thirty-six exposures to a roll. But if the photographer wanted to develop a film that had only been partly exposed, a special film cutter was incorporated by unscrewing a small milled knob on the base of the body and pulling out a long spindle. Inside the closed body this operated a knife that cut through the film. Opening the camera in a darkroom then allowed the photographer to remove the film that had been exposed, whilst leaving the rest of the unexposed film in the cassette.

Ihagee went on to make other models, while rival manufacturers produced their own versions. All the early models utilised waist-level viewfinders, which made them slightly awkward to use and, in truth,

The Contax S was the first 35mm camera with an eye-level viewfinder.

this type of camera didn't play a great part in the coming Second World War. It was only when eye-level viewfinders on 35mm SLRs became the norm shortly after the war, with the introduction of the Contax S, that the 35mm SLR really took off to later play a major role in photography during the Korean War.

The first 16mm camera

Like 35mm before it, 16mm film began life in the movie camera world. The film size first appeared in a still camera with the introduction of the Mini-Fex in 1932.

The body of the camera was as small as to be expected in a subminiature model, measuring just $8 \times 4.5 \times 3.5$cm. But this body was overshadowed by a comparatively huge lens and shutter that would have been more at home on a camera of a much larger format. A viewfinder was mounted at one end of the top of the camera and the film wind at the opposite end. Controls for apertures and shutter speeds, together with the shutter release, were situated on the lens. The 16mm film was unperforated

The Mini-Fex was the first camera to use 16mm miniature film.

and available in paper-backed rolls to take thirty-six 13×18mm size exposures. Several versions of the camera with different shutter/lens combinations were made to suit all pockets.

The Mini-Fex was aimed at the consumer market, but it also marked the genesis of a great many 16mm film spy cameras that would come to prominence during the Cold War that followed the Second World War.

The first motor drive cameras

In the days before digital photography, most film cameras had built-in, battery-driven motor drives to wind the film automatically after each exposure. But cameras incorporating motor drives existed before the electronic age. The difference is that they ran by clockwork. An early example called Le Pascal dated back as far as 1898, and then there were a few other tries at making clockwork-driven motor drives in the 1920s. But the first truly successful camera was the Robot I, made in Germany in 1934.

Compared to the size of previous clockwork-driven models, it was a neat little camera, barely 10cm long, with a large wind knob to tension the clockwork motor on the top plate, alongside the shutter release. The

The Robot I popularised clockwork motor drive cameras.

A Luftwaffe version
of the Robot camera.

viewfinder swivelled through 90 degrees so the photographer could shoot clandestinely at right angles to the subject. The film needed to be pre-loaded into specially designed cassettes, to run from supply cassette to take-up cassette, but in 1939, a new version, called the Robot II, took standard 35mm cassettes.

During the Second World War, special models of the Robot were made for the Luftwaffe (the aerial warfare branch of the combined German Wehrmacht military forces). The advantages of a clockwork motor to advance the film automatically after an exposure also became a tremendous benefit in the later production of spy cameras. Robots continued to be made for many years after the Second World War, as they, and other makes of camera that copied the Robot's basic design, played important roles in espionage activities during the Cold War.

Exposure meters and rangefinders

The difficulties of ascertaining the right combination of shutter speeds and apertures required to give correct exposure were solved to a large extent with the advent of photo-electric exposure meters. These relied on the way a chemical element called selenium generates small amounts of electric current when light strikes it. The higher the level of light, the more the current, which powers a needle to move across a dial to indicate a light value. This is then translated into apertures and shutter speeds to indicate a recommended exposure.

Such meters first appeared in the early 1930s. One English company at the forefront of meter design was Weston, whose earliest model appeared in 1932, and which developed to become the hugely popular Weston Master range in 1939. Known for their ease of use, ruggedness and reliability, these were the meters that went to war.

During the 1930s, exposure meters also began to be built into cameras. The Zeiss Ikon Twin Lens Contaflex was the first in 1936; the Super Kodak Six-20 in 1938 coupled the meter mechanism to the aperture control to automatically set the correct aperture for a chosen shutter speed. Neither of these cameras would have been regarded as rugged enough for use in a war zone.

The first Weston Master
exposure meter.

The second aid to easier camera use concerned measurement of the distance between the camera and the subject, to help focus the lens at the correct distance. The guesswork was taken out of this procedure with the introduction of small accessories known as rangefinders. Most rangefinders used two mirrors – one stationary, the other made to swivel – that viewed the subject through twin windows to overlay two images in a viewfinder eyepiece. As the rangefinder was operated by turning a dial with distances marked on it, the two images moved together and, when they exactly coincided, the subject was in focus. The appropriate distance was then read off the dial. In 1932, the Leica II and the Contax I both

The Leica II (left) and Contax I, two early cameras from 1932 that incorporated rangefinders.

built rangefinders into the cameras. Coupling them to the lens's focusing mechanism meant that adjusting the rangefinder also automatically set the lens focus at the correct distance. Cameras of this type were used extensively in the hostilities that followed.

Photography in the armed forces

In 1937, the War Office formed the Directorate of Public Relations with a remit that included filming and photography. Despite that, and even though army photographers were active during the First World War, there was little activity from the army in the years after that and immediately prior to the Second World War. In fact, it was not until two years into the war that a unit was formed to recruit soldiers with photographic experience for the war effort.

The Royal Air Force, which was formed in 1918 at the end of the First World War, used the years of peace up until the outbreak of the next war to develop new cameras, mostly designed for aerial work. Research into this branch of photography continued after the outbreak of war and throughout the conflict.

Of the three armed forces, the Royal Navy was the most proactive photographically in the years between the wars. During the First World War, the navy used photography to record where shells actually fell in relation to targets at which they were aimed in an effort to improve accuracy. When the war ended, the Admiralty continued that work and, in 1919, set up a Royal Navy Photographic Section.

Ratings recruited for the purpose trained at the Royal Navy School of Photography, combining their naval experience with newly acquired photographic skills in camera usage and darkroom techniques. British-made Thornton Pickard and Sanderson cameras of different sizes were employed for the task, while specialised dial recording cameras, made by the British Houghton-Butcher Manufacturing Company, were used for recording the settings on gunnery systems. These latter cameras were of a particularly unusual design, not unlike twin lens reflexes from during and after the introduction of the Rolleiflex. For instrument recording,

Mark III Dial recording camera, used to record instrument displays as well as conventional photography.

Leica camera equipped with an extra-wide British lens, as advertised by Hugo Meyer in 1928 without actually mentioning the name of the camera.

only the lower lens was used, while shutter tensioning and film wind were effected by tugging on a thin rope wound around a pulley wheel connected to the film roll. Because the camera also had a reflex viewfinder on the top of the body, which received its image via the upper of the camera's two lenses, it could also be used for conventional photography.

Irrespective of the fact that Britain had been at war with Germany not so many years before (and would be again in the near future), the navy also used German Leica cameras. Some were, however, equipped with extra wide aperture British lenses, made by A.O. Roth of London. The same cameras were sold to the general public and advertised as multi-exposure focal plane cameras with f/1.5 lenses.

Movie cameras

Meanwhile, in the civilian world, movie cameras were developing almost as fast as their still camera counterparts, and some of the innovations made during the years between the wars would soon prove indispensable to the next generation of war photographers.

By the end of the First World War, 35mm had become the standard film gauge for movie cameras, but in 1923 two new gauges were introduced in two new movie cameras. One was adopted purely by amateur cinematographers; the other became popular with the kind of professional film makers who operated in the war to come. The amateur gauge was 9.5mm, introduced in France by Charles Pathé, first in a projector for use with commercially available films, and then in a camera to shoot the new film size. Although very popular with amateur cinematographers, 9.5mm was largely ignored by professionals.

But then, the same year that Pathé produced a 9.5mm camera, Kodak introduced a movie camera for 16mm film. The size of the frame on which images were recorded in a 16mm camera was 9.65×7.21mm, against 18×24mm on 35mm film. This meant that a 100ft reel of 16mm gave the same amount of shooting and screen time as a 250ft reel of 35mm. Furthermore, Kodak's new film differed from previous films in another important way. Until then, movie film was usually shot as a negative, which needed to be printed as a positive for projection purposes. The new 16mm system produced a direct positive image on the actual film that was run through the camera, saving time and expense.

The camera that launched 16mm film was called the Cine-Kodak Model A. It was a large, box-shaped camera that measured $22 \times 21 \times 12$cm. A direct vision viewfinder passed through the body and film was driven through the camera by a smooth-turning handle on the side, though an add-on clockwork motor drive soon became available. Pointers and dials for setting apertures and focusing, as well as an indicator to the amount of film used, were all found on the back of the camera where they could be easily seen by the cameraman prior to, or during, filming.

The economies and lower costs that came from using 16mm film and cameras in place of 35mm equipment immediately appealed to amateur cinematographers, but it wasn't long before professional cinematographers also saw the advantages. By the time the Second World

The Cine-Kodak Model A, which introduced 16mm film.

War broke out, 16mm film had established itself as a logical way forward. Although the Cine-Kodak wasn't taken up to any great extent by war photographers, the new 16mm film gauge was adopted by other movie manufacturers, whose cameras were used extensively in the war to come.

The other innovation in movie camera manufacture during these years came in 1932, once again from Kodak with the introduction of a camera called the Cine-Kodak Eight-20. This also took 16mm film, but in smaller reels and with a different method of operation. First it exposed images on half of the film's width. Then, by removing the spools from the camera, turning them over and running the film back again, it exposed a second set of images beside the first. After processing, the film was split

The Cine-Kodak Eight-20, which introduced 8mm film.

down the middle and the two ends joined together. In this way, 25 feet of film in the camera became 50 feet of film for projection. The image size was 4.37×3.28mm, a quarter the size of a 16mm frame. A standard reel of 8mm film gave a four-minute run when shooting at the standard 16 frames per second.

After the Second World War, this new type of film was adopted as the most popular film gauge of all time among amateur movie makers. But 8mm equipment played no real part in the official documentation of the Second World War. The cameras were, however, sometimes taken to war by amateur photographers in the army, navy or air force, and a Cine-Kodak Eight-20 was notably used by an amateur photographer in the navy to film the Battle of the River Plate in South America, the first major naval engagement of the Second World War.

Chapter 8

Focus On: The Ensign Midget

nsign Midget cameras perfectly illustrated how a manufacturer changed its thinking, advertising, marketing and consequently the sales potential of its products to take advantage of the changing times wrought by war. Made by the British Houghton Butcher company and launched in 1934, five years before hostilities began, war was the last thing on the manufacturer's minds as its advertising proclaimed, 'The Camera you wear like a watch'...

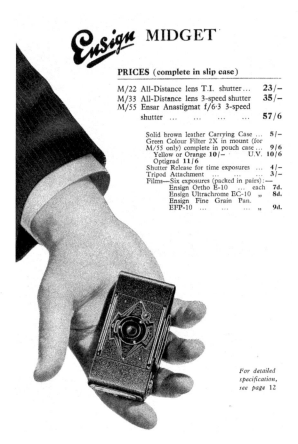

MIDGET

PRICES (complete in slip case)

M/22 All-Distance lens T.I. shutter...	**23/–**	
M/33 All-Distance lens 3-speed shutter	**35/–**	
M/55 Ensar Anastigmat f/6·3 3-speed shutter	**57/6**	

Solid brown leather Carrying Case ...	**5/–**	
Green Colour Filter 2X in mount (for M/55 only) complete in pouch case ...	**9/6**	
Yellow or Orange **10/–**	U.V. **10/6**	
Optigrad **11/6**		
Shutter Release for time exposures ...	**4/–**	
Tripod Attachment	**3/–**	
Films—Six exposures (packed in pairs):—		
Ensign Ortho E-10 ... each	**7d.**	
Ensign Ultrachrome EC-10 ,,	**8d.**	
Ensign Fine Grain Pan. EFP-10 ... ... ,,	**9d.**	

For detailed specification, see page 12

Advertising for the Midget emphasised its small size.

Whether you use a big camera or not, just slip a Midget into your pocket and you need never miss anything of pictorial interest. You won't even know it's in your pocket. Very strongly made. Three-speed shutter, scientifically adjusted lenses giving pin-point definition at all apertures – making perfect enlarging negatives.

With the advent of war, the advertising changed, claiming the Midget to be, 'A remarkable War-Time Camera'…

The Midget is a camera for those who have to consider space. It is a bare half-inch longer than a packet of cigarettes, and no thicker. It goes into a tunic pocket with room to spare. It is essentially the camera for the man in camp. Just the thing to give to a fellow who is called up or to a woman in Service.

As its name implied, the Midget's strong selling point was its size: just $9 \times 4.5 \times 2$cm when folded and only $9 \times 7 \times 6$cm when unfolded with its viewfinders erected ready for shooting. The camera was designed by Swedish engineer Magnus Neill, who had previously designed the Ensignette in 1909, a popular camera whose popularity only waned when the Vest Pocket Kodak was introduced. No doubt Ensign hoped that just as the Vest Pocket Kodak became known as The Soldier's Camera during the First World War, the Midget might become The Soldier's Camera of the Second World War, although unlike the Vest Pocket Kodak when it was initially introduced, the Ensign Midget faced competition from several other miniature cameras.

One reason why small cameras won favour at this time harked back to the launch of the first Leica in 1925. That was the camera that introduced small format negatives sized 24×36mm on 35mm film. Such small dimensions were treated with suspicion in the early days, but by the mid-1930s they had become far more acceptable. One problem, however, lay in the fact that 35mm film was sold in cassettes with enough for thirty-six exposures. Many considered this to be too many pictures needing to be shot on a film before it could be developed. With that in mind, manufacturers began making small cameras that took their own unique sizes of tiny roll film to give negative sizes approximate to those from

Folded and unfolded, the pocket-size Ensign Midget.

a Leica, but with far fewer shots to a roll. The Ensign Midget was one of the cameras that followed that thinking. It shot six pictures on E10 size film, which cost 6d (2.5p) a roll, and although the camera was much smaller than a Leica, the size of the image it produced, at 30 × 40mm, was actually a little larger. There were five models.

The Midget cameras

Neill's intention was to make a camera that folded to a clean design that left no extraneous bulges, bumps, lumps, levers or knobs. The black rippled body was made from pressed steel with chrome fittings. It was unfolded by gripping two serrated panels top and bottom of the lens panel and pulling forward until metal struts click-stopped into position. The Ensign Midget name was emblazoned each side of the lens in an attractive art deco styling. The camera was equipped with two viewfinders. The first was a small reflecting brilliant type, which, when the camera was held in the vertical position, viewed the subject through an aperture in the lens panel. For horizontal pictures, the same viewfinder folded out from behind the panel on a short arm. For eye-level view finding, a metal frame double-folded onto the top of the lens panel to line up with a sight that swivelled up from the rear of the body.

This style was common to two models launched at the same time in 1934. Initially they were called the A/N and the A/D, the former

The three main models of the Ensign Midget: left to right, the Model 55, Model 33 and Model 22.

having a full range of apertures and a focusing lens, the latter with only two apertures and a fixed focus lens. Later the camera names were changed to the Model 55 and Model 33, an indication of their prices in shillings (there were twenty shillings to a pound in Britain's pre-decimal currency). In 1935, a new, simplified version was produced with the lens focus, apertures and shutter speed all fixed at single settings. It was called the Model 22 and sold for twenty-two shillings. Also, in 1935, to celebrate the silver jubilee of King George V and Queen Mary in May of that year, silver versions were issued of the Model 33 and Model 55 cameras.

The Silver models of the cameras produced for the silver jubilee of King George V and Queen Mary in 1935.

The Midget on the home front

Soldiers were not the only market at which Ensign aimed its advertising during the Second World War. Those at home were also encouraged to buy the cameras for different wartime purposes…

> Some people are making war-time diaries with these Midgets, taking snaps of subjects like children going to school with their gas masks, cars bearing war-time notices, men digging for victory on allotments, or of someone pasting strips of paper on the window. All these little war-time incidents make photographs which will be treasured later on. These cameras are splendid for capturing that sort of thing. It is an idea. Keep an Ensign Midget war-time diary. The photographs will be wonderfully interesting in the years when war is a thing of the past. Buy a Midget and start now.

Having covered soldiers and civilians alike, Ensign also went on to target children, experienced photographers and, really, just about anyone to whom they might stand a chance of selling it…

> Boys and girls like the almost secret proportions of the Midget too. It is a camera that has an appeal to the experienced photographer as well, because, with a Midget in his waistcoat pocket, he need never miss an opportunity. It is a camera that anybody, man or woman, can carry always without the slightest inconvenience. The Midget has overcome the bugbear of bulk.

Production of the Ensign Midget halted in 1940 as Houghton Butcher went over to war work. On the night of 24/25 September that year, the company's premises in London's High Holborn were wiped out in a German bombing raid. Production of the Ensign Midget did not resume after the Second World War.

Chapter 9

The Second World War

The detailed reasons that led to the outbreak of the Second World War were many and complex and it is not the intention of a book such as this to analyse these causes in detail. Events and movements such as the rise of Italian fascism from the 1920s onwards and the rise of militarism in Japan with its invasion of China in the 1930s would not have greatly affected the average person in Britain. But then, in 1933, came the political takeover in Germany by the Nazi Party and its aggressive foreign policy that culminated in the invasion of Poland on 1 September 1939. Two days later, on 3 September, Britain declared war on Germany. To go from peace to war in such a short pace of time

Dalmeyer lenses play their part in cameras required for war and peace in a 1944 advertisement.

left the country ill-prepared in many ways – including those in which cameras and photography in general were about to change both military and civilian lives.

Camera technology had come on apace in the years between the wars. Even so, in Britain there was a significant gap between the declaration of war and any significant start of serious photographic activity in the armed forces.

The Royal Navy formed a photographic branch that placed ratings with photographic experience on board ships to shoot pictures of flight deck incidents on aircraft carriers, battle damage and public relations photography of ships' crews posed on deck, which the sailors were allowed to send home once the pictures had been approved by censors. At the outbreak of war, the British Army already had a Directorate of Public Relations, whose remit included filming and photography, though not in the field. With the outbreak of war, the Directorate appointed an official War Office Cinematographer, but an order from the Secretary of State prohibiting photography of military subjects made life for any photographer or cinematographer, official or otherwise, somewhat difficult, resulting in a lack of newsreel pictures of army activities in these early days.

As the Second World War broke out, of the three armed forces, the Royal Air Force was the one best equipped photographically, where cameras were used chiefly for aerial reconnaissance.

Aerial cameras

F24

Conceived by the Royal Aircraft Establishment at Farnborough, and manufactured by the Williamson Manufacturing Company in north-west London, the F24 comprised a body with a focal plane shutter that could be set between 1/100 and 1/1000 second and an f/2.9 Dallmeyer Pentac lens in a cone on the front of the camera. It shot pictures 5×5 inches on 5-inch wide rolls of film that had a capacity for up to 250 exposures. Although several similar, and often a great deal larger, cameras were used by the Royal Air Force during the Second World War, it was the F24 that became the workhorse, adapted for specialist uses with a range

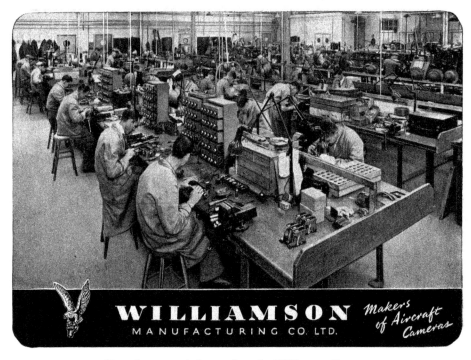

Aircraft cameras being made at the Williamson factory.

The F-24 camera that was installed in many aircraft.

of different lenses. During the war, F24 cameras were installed in aircraft that included the Avenger, Blenheim, Catalina, Corsair, Halifax, Hellcat, Hudson, Hurricane, Lancaster, Liberator, Lysander, Maryland, Mitchell, Mosquito, Mustang, Spitfire, Stinson, Stirling, Sunderland and Wellington. In 1942, the camera was further developed as the F52, whose image format was a massive $8\frac{1}{2} \times 7$ inches, using film magazines that could shoot up to 500 exposures.

F95

W. Vinten Ltd. began in London during 1910 making equipment for colour cinema processes. In the First World War, the company made aircraft parts and then aircraft cameras. During the Second World War, Vinten went on to produce reconnaissance cameras for the Royal Air Force. The F95 was manufactured for installation in Canberra aircraft,

The Vinten F95 Mark 6 aerial reconnaissance camera used by the RAF during the Second World War.

where it was mounted in the forward camera bay in a fixed and immobile position. For that reason, the whole aircraft had to be moved to frame the picture. For this purpose a black cross was drawn using a wax marker pencil onto the inside of the aircraft's double-glazed canopy, with a second cross marked on the outside. When the pilot lined up the aircraft so that the two crosses coincided, the camera lens was aimed correctly at the chosen subject.

K-20

In America, the K-20 was manufactured by the Folmer Graflex Corporation in Rochester and put into service from 1941 to 1946. The all-metal camera was used handheld, loaded with roll film 5¼ inches wide and anything from 20 to 200 feet long on which it shot 4 × 5-inch images. A vacuum system was used to keep the film flat during exposure. The camera was loaded onto bomber planes, enabling the pilot to shoot low-altitude pictures of targets such as enemy missile launch sites. One

The K-20, developed in America.

The cover of the first issue of the American *Camera Comics* shows how cameras like the
K-20 were seen, and somewhat romanticised, in October 1944.

of these cameras was mounted in the tail gunner position of the Boeing B-29 Superfortress bomber, from which the first atomic bomb was dropped on Hiroshima towards the end of the war.

Williamson Pistol Camera

This was a handheld model made in 1933 for use in light aircraft or on the ground. The camera was contained within an aluminium cone with a viewfinder on the top and a handle below that incorporated a trigger mechanism to fire the shutter. It shot 6 × 9cm images on glass plates, roll film or film packs. The standard lens with which it was equipped could be interchanged for a telephoto. The camera was made by Williamson in London.

Williamson Pistol Camera.

WILLIAMSON PISTOL CAMERA
For Air or Ground Snapshots

● Pistol Camera, complete for use in the air or on the ground, fitted with Ross Xpres F/4.5 5.3'' lens, six single dark slides, one film pack adapter, focussing mount and screen in leather carrying case with lock, key and sling
£25.0.0

● Pistol Camera, complete for use in the air, fitted with Dallmeyer 5.3'' F/4.5 lens, six single dark slides, one film pack adapter, in leather carrying case with lock, key and sling
£19.5.0

The Williamson All-metal ever-set Louvre type shutter is situated immediately behind the lens and is independent of it, thus enabling a telephoto lens to be interchanged with a standard one if desired.

Other features of this convenient camera are the fine balance and the large trigger guard, which enables a thickly-gloved hand to operate the camera with ease. In the air or on the ground, the Williamson "Pistol" Camera is equally efficient. Standard films or plates, size 3¼ x 2¼ (6 x 9 cm.) are obtainable from all dealers.

LOUVRE SHUTTER SPEEDS UP TO 1/200th OF A SECOND

Williamson Manufacturing Co. Ltd.
Makers of F8, F24, G22, G28 Cameras.

LITCHFIELD GARDENS, WILLESDEN GREEN, LONDON, N.W.10
Telephone: WILLESDEN 0073-0074   Telegrams: KINETOGRAM, WILLROAD, LONDON   Cables: KINETOGRAM, LONDON

How the Pistol camera was advertised.

Aerial Komlosy camera

When it was introduced in Britain in 1941, this camera's main use was for reconnaissance. It was designed to be handheld as its operator stood at an aircraft's open fuselage door. The camera's major controls, including

Aerial Komlosy camera shot 6 × 6cm exposures on 70mm film.

a large lever at the base for advancing the film, were over-large and somewhat exaggerated to enable airmen to operate it more easily while wearing aircrew inner gloves and leather gauntlets. The camera shot forty 6 × 6cm pictures on 70mm wide film, which contained sprockets top and bottom in the manner of the smaller 35mm film as an aid to accurate film advance between exposures.

Luftwaffe Handkammer

Germany's answer to cameras like the British F24 and the American K-20 was this air reconnaissance camera, made to be used handheld. It was manufactured by Fritz Völk Mechanische Werkstätten in Berlin in 1941. The 80mm wide film was pre-loaded into interchangeable magazines to make changing film faster. A similar camera, called the Reihenbildner, had a motorised film wind.

The Luftwaffe Handkammer was Germany's equivalent of the British F-24 and American K-20.

Williamson G45

Cameras were not just placed in aeroplanes for reconnaissance purposes. They were also there to record the accuracy or otherwise of a pilot's shooting during air-to-air combat. One of the best known cameras used for this purpose was the G45, manufactured by Williamson in London. The camera comprised a long, flat metal boxlike body with a lens at one end. A hatch in the body opened at the top and a flap was let down at the side to insert a cartridge of 16mm cine film, driven through the camera by an electric motor, powered from the aircraft. From 1939, the G45 was fitted to Spitfires and Hurricanes, then to other aircraft as the war progressed. The camera was synchronised to start filming as the aeroplane's guns were fired to make a photographic record of the accuracy of the pilot's shooting. Each cartridge contained 25 feet of film, which could be shot at sixteen, eighteen or twenty-four frames per second. When the aeroplane returned to base, the film was quickly processed to assess the pilot's prowess on that particular mission.

The Williamson G45 that was fitted to Spitfires and Hurricanes.

Advertisements for the Eagle range of aerial cameras made by Williamson.

Williamson was at the forefront of promoting cameras for aerial photography, even to the extent of mentioning, in a 1943 advertisement, General Thomas Ludwig Werner Freiherr von Fritsch, Commander-in-Chief of the German Army from 1933 to 1938. Before the outbreak of war,

Aerial photography over Germany as seen through the eyes of a now unknown cartoonist from RAF Leeming.

the German general was quoting as saying, 'The military organisation with the best photo reconnaissance will win the next war.' To prove it, the Williamson advertisement showed newspaper clippings with headlines that stated...

Camera shows vast bomb damage in Germany
RAF 'eyes' are best in world
Cameras helped win Tunisia
Tirpitz found and photographed
Lone pilot photographs Hitler line secrets
Infra-red camera beats the observer's eye in spotting camouflage
   from the air
RAF pilots film Europe from the sub-stratosphere

Flash photography at night

Aerial cameras were not exclusive to daytime use. Under the heading 'Snapshots at night that mean bad days for the Japs', a 1940s Kodak advertisement explained...

It's midnight and away 'upstairs' our reconnaissance photographers dodge flak and night fighters to snap pictures of enemy territory. Light's no problem. They turn night into day with a giant flash bomb. It's big brother to the newspaper photographer's flash bulb; it weighs 52 pounds, carries 26 pounds of flash powder, at the peak of its flash gives a billion candlepower. The flash bomb's fuse is set to explode and ignite the flash powder at a point behind the plane. The explosion works a photoelectric cell, which clicks the camera shutter.

According to the advertisement, the first successful flash-bomb photographs had been made by the US Army working with Kodak technicians as far back as 1924. The company was also quick to point out that Kodak's aerial lenses and films played a large part in reconnaissance raids at night. These and other products, it was claimed, helped give American armed forces 'the best war photography in the world'.

Snapshots at night that mean bad days for the Japs

BOMB RELEASE POINT

BOMB EXPLODES

PICTURE AREA

IT'S MIDNIGHT and away "upstairs" our reconnaissance photographers dodge flak and night fighters to snap pictures of enemy territory. Light's no problem. They turn night into day with a giant flash bomb. It's big brother to the newspaper photographer's flash bulb; it weighs 52 pounds, carries 26 pounds of flash powder, at the peak of its flash gives a billion candlepower.

The flash bomb's fuse is set to explode and ignite the flash powder at a point behind the plane. The explosion works a photoelectric cell, which clicks the camera shutter.

The first successful flash-bomb photographs were made by the U. S. Army working with Kodak's experts over Rochester, N. Y., in 1924. Kodak aerial lenses and Kodak Films have had a large share in making night photographic raids a regular part of aerial reconnaissance. Scores of other Kodak products have helped give our Armed Forces the best war photography in the world.

EASTMAN KODAK COMPANY
Rochester, N. Y.

YOUR POSTWAR FLASH CAMERA

Here's one camera you'll want right after the war...the Six-20 Flash Brownie. Capable daylight snapshooter—with Flashholder makes swell Photoflash shots at night — indoors or out. A lot of camera for a little money.

Kodak

A Kodak advertisement for its flash-bomb photography.

The Army Film and Photographic Unit

At the start of the war, the British were slow to appreciate the value of photography. Not so German forces who, right from the start, recognised the importance of using cameras to depict military conflict, as well as giving soldiers a way to keep in contact with their families. In this way they boosted the morale of their troops. In controlling the way photographs were taken they could also disguise any negative aspects that might become apparent. It was all good propaganda.

The British, on the other hand, with the Ministry of Information's censorship of publicity related to military and civil actions, failed to understand the potential benefits of photographic propaganda and consequently the way the British forces were perceived overseas. This was especially true in America, whose troops were yet to enter the war, and where the German propaganda machine depicted that country's military in a better light than the British. In an effort to at least partially

The work of Allied photographic units is celebrated in a 1945 advertisement for Taylor-Hobson lenses.

correct this, in October 1941, two months before America entered the war, the Army Film and Photographic Unit (AFPU) was set up in Britain to record military events concerning British and Commonwealth armies. Its members were not civilian war correspondents, as had often been the case in the past, but recruits from the ranks of the British Army, who were sent for photographic training at Pinewood Film Studios in Buckinghamshire, where they learned the art of using fully manual equipment without the benefit of any of the automation that would later become the norm in all cameras.

On graduation from Pinewood, and with the rank of sergeant bestowed upon them, AFPU photographers were assigned to units in pairs: one to shoot cine film, the other to shoot stills. Because they were soldiers first and photographers second, they were already trained in field craft and weapon handling. Along with their cameras, the operatives carried .38 calibre Wembley Mark IV revolvers and were issued with Royal Armoured Corps steel helmets.

They also carried notebooks in which they recorded details of the pictures taken, the relevant pages then attached to film that was sent back to London for processing. Within reason, they were free to film and photograph each unit's activities in any way they saw fit.

The search for cameras

At the start of operations, the British Army was ill-prepared for the number of cameras actually needed, and from where they might be obtained. The fact was that, while British cameras had held a good solid reputation in the early years of photography, they had gradually lost ground after the First World War. By 1939 and the outbreak of the Second World War, the country that led the field photographically was the very country on which Britain had declared war: Germany.

Politically, the British Army could not import cameras from the enemy, although it was possible to obtain German cameras at low cost via Turkey. Luckily, the rising popularity of German photographic equipment from around the mid-1920s onwards meant there were a lot of photographers, both amateur and professional, within Britain who already owned top-class German equipment. All that was necessary was for them to be

ii   THE MINIATURE CAMERA MAGAZINE   December, 1941

R. G. LEWIS OFFERS THE FOLLOWING BARGAINS IN MINIATURE CAMERAS, ENLARGERS AND ACCESSORIES

No Purchase Tax. No Hire Purchase. All prices quoted are rock-bottom ones for cash, or cash and part exchange. First-class exchange allowances given on all types of miniature equipment.

In addition to our incomparable stocks of miniature bargains at Shrewsbury, we now have a huge assortment of all kinds of miniature cameras, enlargers and accessories at 202, High Holborn. London customers in need of a Leica and Contax equipment are advised to enquire for this first at High Holborn, as our stocks of apparatus of this type are now by far the largest in London.

LEICAS:

CONTAXES:

OTHER MINIATURES WITH COUPLED RANGEFINDERS:

SPECIAL OFFER OF BRAND NEW SUPER-SPORT "A" CAMERAS (MODEL 1 BLACK):

EXAKTAS:

OTHER MINIATURE REFLEXES:

MISCELLANEOUS MINIATURES:

DEVELOPING TANKS

DE-LUXE EVER-READY CASES

UNIVERSAL COPYING EQUIPMENT

RE-LOADABLE CASSETTES FOR LEICA, CONTAX AND OTHER 35-MM. FILM USERS

R. G. LEWIS, LTD., 5, Claremont Bank, Shrewsbury
(TO WHICH ALL LETTERS AND PARCELS SHOULD BE ADDRESSED)

December, 1941   THE MINIATURE CAMERA MAGAZINE   I

WANTED FOR THE BRITISH ARMY

We have been instructed to collect immediately for use by the Army, all available Super Ikontas, Models 530/16 and 532/16. If you have such a camera for disposal, please allow us to purchase it, and as the need is urgent, customers are asked to send such instruments without delay, either to Shrewsbury or to Holborn, enclosing with them a note stating the price required. We are, of course, quite willing to quote a purchase figure, either after inspection of the camera, or receipt of its description, but we are very concerned with the time factor, as these instruments must be in without delay. This is a unique opportunity to put your camera to national service. All cameras received will be passed on by us to the Army authorities without delay. Cheques in settlement will be sent off by return of post.

ALSO WANTED

Miniature Equipment of all kinds. As the only firm specialising exclusively in Miniature Cameras, our prices for these are obviously the highest. We urgently require for firms engaged on National work, R.A.F. stations, etc., Leicas and Contaxes and all telephoto and wide-angle lenses for these. Special accessories, such as contameters, universal finders and copying equipment are also in great demand, and in most cases we are paying in excess of full list prices for these. In addition to Contax and Leica equipment, we wish to buy and are paying exceptional prices for Rolleiflexes, Super Ikontas, Exaktas, Makinas (Model IIS), Reflex Korelles and Primarflexes.

London Showroom : - - 202, HIGH HOLBORN, W.C.1
Shrewsbury Showroom : - 38, CASTLE STREET.   Tel. 3492

A December 1941 photographic magazine advertisement for R.G. Lewis shows the kind of German cameras still being sold, as well as an appeal for readers to donate their photographic equipment for the war cause.

persuaded to part with it. Augmenting this, there were still a few British photographic manufacturers capable of delivering the goods, and there was Kodak in America. So the call went out for cameras.

The first two pages of the December 1941 issue of *The Miniature Camera Magazine* were taken up by an advertisement for R.G. Lewis, one of the country's largest photographic dealers at the time. The briefest glance at the cameras being sold by the dealer seemed to contradict the fact that Britain was at war with the country that made the vast majority of what was on sale. Names like Leica, Contax, Zeiss Ikon, Agfa, Exakta, Rolleiflex, Rolleicord and Voigtländer dominated the pages – and all of them German. Taking up the top half of the second page of the advertisement, there was a plea from the dealer, which read...

WANTED FOR THE BRITISH ARMY

We have been instructed to collect immediately for use by the Army, all available Super Ikontas, Models 530/16 and 532/16. If you have such a camera for disposal, please allow us to purchase it, and as the need is urgent, customers are asked to send such instruments without delay, either to Shrewsbury or to Holborn, enclosing with them a note stating the price required. We are, of course, quite willing to quote a purchase figure, either after inspection of the camera, or receipt of its description, but we are very concerned with the time factor, as these instruments must be in without delay. This is a unique opportunity to put your camera to national service. All cameras received will be passed on by us to the Army authorities without delay. Cheques in settlement will be sent by return of post.

ALSO WANTED

Miniature Equipment of all kinds. As the only firm specialising exclusively in Miniature Cameras, our prices for these are obviously the highest. We urgently require for firms engaged on National work, RAF stations, etc, Leicas and Contaxes and all telephoto and wide-angle lenses for these. Special accessories such as contameters, universal finders and copying equipment are also in great demand, and in most cases we are paying in excess of full list prices for these. In addition to Contax and Leica equipment, we wish to buy and are paying exceptional prices for Rolleiflexes, Super Ikontas, Exaktas, Makinas, Reflex Korelles and Primarflexes.

The call for cameras continued in the years that followed. In January 1943, *The Amateur Photographer*, one of the world's best respected and bestselling weekly photography magazines, gave over its whole front cover to an advertisement for Wallace Heaton, a well-known London-based dealer. The picture that dominated the advertisement was a winner in the photo dealer's weekly photographic competition, showing a policeman holding his hand up in the traditional 'police stop' gesture. The words that were added were more about the war effort: 'Halt! Send us your Leica or Contax now.'

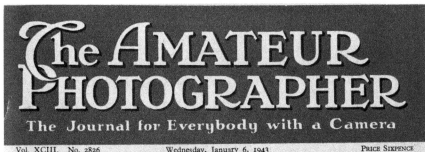

This photograph won a prize in Wallace Heaton's weekly competition, by—

G. R. HINKS, MANCHESTER, 19

Halt!

Send your Leica or Contax now

to

Wallace Heaton Ltd.

(See inside announcement.)

The front cover of *The Amateur Photographer* for January 1943, with its plea for Leica and Contax cameras.

The cameras that went to war

The cameras that went into world war conflict the second time around were a lot more sophisticated than those used in the previous world war. Most of them, obtained by the government through various channels, including donations from the public, were issued by the AFPU for official military use. But many were used unofficially, as policing the rules set up to prevent soldiers taking cameras into battle proved impossible. Today the snapshots, as opposed to professional photographs, taken by many of these soldier amateur photographers, have proved to be of as much interest as the professional officially taken pictures. Civilian photo journalists also found their way into war zones and their pictures today also contribute a great deal to what is known of the war. Here is a list of cameras – many of which were issued by the AFPU – that were used both officially and unofficially during the Second World War.

Super Ikonta 530/16 & 532/16

Carl Zeiss Jena was an optical company that made high precision lenses for microscopes and other scientific instruments. The company did not make cameras, but did make lenses for many top camera manufacturers. When the First World War ended in 1918 it left the German economy in serious need of repair, and the only way many manufacturers survived was by amalgamating. If Zeiss was to continue to make and sell camera lenses, something needed to be done about the ailing camera manufacturing industry, and so a Zeiss holding company was set up to orchestrate the coming together of four major camera manufacturers – Ica, Contessa-Nettel, Ernemann and Goerz – to form Zeiss Ikon, which set up business in Dresden in 1926. Between them, those four companies had previously made almost every type of camera and, from this melting pot, came many camera names that became legendary. Ikonta and Super Ikonta cameras were among the most prestigious.

Although 35mm film had been around since 1925, and had by now attained a growing respectability for its ability to produce quality pictures from such a small format, there was still a faction that looked upon 35mm as something more for amateurs than professionals. As a result, two of the most popular cameras issued by the AFPU were these two models of the Super Ikonta B, made by Zeiss Ikon. They were described by the

Zeiss Ikon Super Ikonta, model 530/16.

AFPU as being the best and handiest in action, and were used prolifically during the D-Day landings.

The specifications of the two cameras were very similar. Both were folding models, in which a bed dropped down from a flat boxlike body, with lenses that self-erected on bellows. Each took 120 size roll film to produce eleven 6 × 6cm square negatives on each roll. Various lenses were available, but all were fixed and not interchangeable. Shutter speeds and apertures were set manually around the rims of the lenses, but there was no inbuilt method of determining exposure; that would have needed the use of an exposure meter or, more often than not, the experienced intuition of the photographer. To aid focusing, the cameras had coupled rangefinders. In the 530/16 model the rangefinder was viewed through a window beside the viewfinder; in the 532/16, the rangefinder was built into the viewfinder to speed up focusing and shooting.

Using the cameras could be a slow process compared to some other types, particularly 35mm cameras, but the quality produced by the Zeiss lenses, coupled with the size of the negatives, ensured excellence.

Leica IIIa

Since the launch of the first Leica in 1925, the camera had gradually evolved. By the time the IIIa incarnation was launched in 1935, it had become a well-respected, beautifully made, highly reliable camera with an interchangeable lens range that offered focal lengths from wide-angle to telephoto, all coupled to a rangefinder to aid focusing. The IIIa was the first Leica to offer a top shutter speed of 1/1000 second, which made it more versatile for action photography; the slow shutter speeds, attainable via a separate knob on the front of the body, went down to a full one second.

The camera took 35mm film and produced thirty-six exposures to each cassette, but Leicas of this time had an awkward way of loading film through the base, which made it slower to reload in action. As well as a vast range of lenses, Leica cameras also accepted a great many accessories including a reflex viewfinder announced the same year as the Leica IIIa, which, when equipped with the correct lens, turned the camera into a

The IIIa was the current model of Leica available at the outbreak of the war.

A Visoflex accessory with suitable lens turned the Leica IIIa into a single lens reflex.

single lens reflex. The Leica IIIa was the most produced of all Leica cameras up until the Second World War. It was a favourite with war correspondents.

Contax II

In 1929, it was decided to rationalise the Zeiss Ikon range, which was too full of similar cameras previously made by the four different manufacturers that came together to make up the new company. At the same time it was decided to produce a new kind of camera not previously seen in the Zeiss stable. The camera would take 35mm film and, when launched, would stand as the first rival to the Leica. After two short years, the new camera arrived on the market and was called the Contax, which went on to be upgraded as the Contax II in 1936.

It was the Contax II that was distributed by the AFPU. This was a very attractive camera whose body was finished in satin chrome, which might not have been an advantage if a soldier was attempting to camouflage

The Contax II (left) and Contax III 35mm rangefinder cameras from Zeiss Ikon.

himself and his equipment. Nevertheless, its quality could not be denied. The lens was interchangeable on a bayonet mount and, at the time of its launch, lenses were available from wide-angle to telephoto. The range was extended after the war. A small thumbwheel that protruded from the top of the body to fall easily under a finger of the right hand was turned to rotate the lens for focusing, and this was coupled to a rangefinder in the viewfinder to aid accuracy. The shutter release was in the centre of the film wind knob. The camera produced thirty-six exposures to each cassette of 35mm film. Everything about the design made the Contax II intuitively easy to use. Shortly after its launch, a new model was announced called the Contax III. It was similar in most respects to its predecessor, except that it had a built-in exposure meter to measure light and help set the correct shutter speeds and apertures. The advantages of having a meter built into the body made this the better camera, but it probably saw less service with the military than did the Contax II.

The camera was used a great deal by assault units who, after photographic training, were issued with Contaxes for use in capturing intelligence ahead of the advance of Allied armies.

Rolleiflex Automat

Rolleiflex cameras, made in Germany by the Franke Heidecke company, first came to the market in 1928 with the launch of new and improved models in the years to follow. By this time, the latest camera in the range was the Automat, first made in 1937. Like all Rolleiflex cameras, it was a twin lens reflex, taking the shape of a tall box with two lenses, one above the other. The lower lens shot the picture, while the upper lens

The Rolleiflex Automat twin lens reflex.

reflected its image onto a large screen under a hood at the top of the body. Although it could be used at eye level, the conventional method was to hold the camera at waist level while looking down into the hooded viewfinder screen.

It shot twelve 6 × 6cm exposures on 120 film and, with a special adapter called a Rolleikin, it could be used with 35mm film to shoot thirty-six exposures. An underwater housing was also available. Rolleiflex cameras were known for the quality of their engineering and optics. On the plus side, because they did not have to be unfolded before shooting, they were ready for action much faster. For ease and speed of use, the Rolleiflex was ahead of the Super Ikonta, but behind 35mm cameras like the Contax and Leica. Even so, Rolleiflex twin lens reflex cameras were more likely to have been used for recording relatively static subjects, such as wounded troops on the way back from a battle rather than the action of the battle itself.

Ensign Commando

Ensign cameras were made in England by the Houghton company and this was one of the few British cameras issued to troops, albeit not until close to the end of the war in 1945. Many military cameras were adapted from civilian models, but the Commando, as its name implies, was the

The Ensign Commando, made for the military, was later adopted for civilian use.

opposite. It was made as a military camera, and then later adapted for civilian consumer use. The Commando was a self-erecting folding camera with a coupled rangefinder, but an unusual method of focusing. In most cameras, the lens was moved backwards and forwards in relation to the film, which remained static. In the Commando, the lens remained static, while the film moved backwards and forwards for focusing purposes. The camera took 120 size roll film, offering a choice of twelve 6 × 6cm or sixteen 4.5 × 6cm images, the latter produced by folding two flaps across the film plane and use of the twin red window system.

Bessa I

Made by Voigtländer in Germany and first seen in 1931, this was one of the more basic cameras issued by the AFPU. Its strength was that it took large 6 × 9cm images, and yet folded into a compact package that could fit easily into a pocket. The optics and mechanical aspects of the camera were first class. Its main drawback was the small viewfinder attached to the side of the lens, which was used at waist level and too small to accurately frame a subject at speed, although a fold-up metal viewfinder on the side of the body used at eye level was better suited.

The Bessa I, a folding camera from the German Voigtländer company.

Kodak 35 Military

Even in 1938 when it was launched, the Kodak 35 looked old fashioned, chiefly because the viewfinder comprised little more than a couple of appendages that folded up from the top plate with a front and rear sight for the photographer to squint through. That aside, it was a well-made little camera with a Bakelite body and bright metal fittings whose technical specification was well up to the standards required for straightforward photography without any frills. In 1941, Kodak introduced a military version in a drab olive colour, which was used mostly by the American army.

The military version of the Kodak 35.

Argus C3

This was another American camera issued to that country's military, which, because it contained a built-in rangefinder coupled to the lens for accurate focusing, proved to be more popular than the smaller Kodak 35. The C3 earned itself a nickname of The Brick, because of its square-ended, rugged design. It was a 35mm model with an unusual focusing

The Argus C3, popularly known as The Brick.

mechanism that involved a wheel engraved with a focusing scale on the front of the body, geared to the lens via a second gear wheel. Shutter speeds were set around another dial also on the front of the body and apertures were changed by a ring around the lens. It all added up to a rugged little camera that was easy to use, unless accessories like a filter or lens hood were attached, which made the apertures impossible to adjust. For this, a small Y-shaped accessory was supplied to fit onto the aperture ring beneath the filter or hood and with a protruding arm with which apertures could be adjusted. The accessory was small, fiddly to fit and very easy to lose. A dedicated bulb flashgun was available.

Retina II

While it was generally becoming accepted at this time that the 35mm film format could produce quality images, it was also acknowledged that 35mm cameras – chiefly in the shape of Leicas and Contaxes – were expensive to produce and buy. Then, in 1934, Kodak introduced the Retina, a folding camera like a miniature version of the company's earlier folding roll film models, but made to take 35mm film. While that camera

The Retina II was cheaper to buy than a Leica or Contax but still produced quality images on 35mm film.

evolved with several variations on the original theme, the Retina II was introduced in 1937 with the advantage of a coupled rangefinder.

Folding to a neat package that measured only $11.5 \times 8 \times 3$cm, it was small enough to slip into a pocket, yet offered the technical specification and the kind of picture quality associated with its far more expensive counterparts. The camera was made at Kodak's German factory in Stuttgart, but production was interrupted in 1941 when the German government requisitioned the factory for war work. Then the plant was bombed by the Allies in 1944. But as soon as the war ended in 1945, production began again as Stuttgart fell into the American sector of West Germany and Retina cameras were made for the American Military Post-Exchange System, a type of retail store located on American military bases around the world. Retina cameras continued to be made through the 1950s, 1960s and even as late as the 1970s.

Speed Graphic

By the time of the Second World War, the Speed Graphic, which had been introduced by the American Graflex company in 1912 and had already been through the Fist World War, was still a popular workhorse for press photographers. It also retained its use with the American Signal Corps photographers who used it on a daily basis. It was a big and heavy plate camera, which required glass plates to be changed between exposures. Although more suitable for use on a tripod, eye-level viewfinders made it relatively easy to use hand-held. Even so, it could not compare with 35mm cameras like the Leica and Contax, or even the folding roll film models

The Speed Graphic, still popular in the Second World War.

How Graflex cameras were advertised during the Second World War.

such as the Super Ikontas. But the quality of the images it produced could not be disputed. In America a military version of the Speed Graphic was issued to soldiers as part of a set, which included a bulb flashgun, cable release, filters, lens hood, six glass plates, a lens cleaning cloth and wooden tripod all contained in a partitioned fibre chest.

Kodak Medalist

By 1941, the Speed Graphic was really beginning to look primitive and was replaced that year by the Kodak Medalist, which had the advantage of being somewhat smaller and taking 620 size roll film. The cube-shaped camera was rugged, heavy and seemingly built like a tank. Although still a little awkward to use, it was a lot easier and faster in operation than the previous Speed Graphic and proved to be an extremely versatile camera. It was issued to American soldiers mostly for colour photography. The first 1941 model was upgraded after the war in 1946. (More about this unusual camera in the following chapter.)

JAP DIVE BOMBER TAGGED BY ANTIAIRCRAFT
FIRE FROM A NAVY CARRIER

CIAL UNITED STATES NAVY PHOTOGRAPH

His battle station's behind a KODAK

• He's one of the Navy's combat cameramen. There's a "show" on, and he's right in the thick of things —with a Kodak Medalist glued to his eye.

The Medalist has been serving at sea ever since the war began. Sturdy as a battle wagon, compact as a submarine, the Medalist looks and acts "Navy." Its lens is the finest ever made for this type of camera. With shutter speeds down to 1/400 of a second, it catches the split-second action of American-style blitz warfare in wonderfully clear, dramatic pictures.

Perhaps you won't need all the "high power" of a camera like Kodak Medalist even when Victory makes it available again to the public. But for a model capable of recording young America's

**KODAK MEDALIST—
RECORDER OF VICTORY**

sports and hobbies and outings, you certainly want to look up the Brownie Reflex, Synchro Model, for day or night snapshots.

Your Postwar Favorite?

Brownie Reflex, Synchro Model, with Flasholder for inexpensive batteries and "midget" bulbs, is ready for service any hour of the twenty-four. Snap open the hooded view-finder, spot your subject in full picture size (1⅝ x 1⅝ inches), and push the button—fixed focus catches any view from 6 feet to "infinity." It's a sturdy, handy camera. At your dealer's after the war is over . . .
Eastman Kodak Company, Rochester 4, New York.

Kodak

A 1940s American advertisement proclaims the advantages of using the Medalist for naval combat photography.

Minox

Thanks largely to film and television, the Minox has become recognised as the archetypal spy camera. It was about the size of an index finger, with a telescopic body that extended to reveal the viewfinder and uncover the lens at the same time. The action of opening and closing the body also advanced the film, which was 9.5mm wide and produced tiny images 8 × 11mm. The cameras are mostly known for being made in West Germany after the war, but the very first model was produced in Latvia in 1937, the brainchild of photographer, photo dealer and eventually camera designer Walter Zapp. It was known as the Riga Minox, after the town where it was conceived.

During the Second World War, it was this early Minox that was taken up by the Special Operations Executive formed in Britain in 1940 from the amalgamation of three other secret organisations. The Executive's purpose was to aid resistance movements in occupied Europe, while conducting espionage, sabotage and reconnaissance operations. Known in some quarters as Churchill's Secret Army, few were aware of the organisation's existence. Later, when the war ended and production of new models of the Minox was shifted to West Germany, the camera won acclaim for the ease with which it could be used clandestinely during the Cold War that followed the Second World War. (More about this camera in a later chapter.)

The original Minox camera that was used for espionage work in the Second World War.

Kine Exakta

Although the Kine Exakta (covered in detail in a previous chapter on *The Years Between the Wars*) was recognised as the first 35mm single lens reflex, it wasn't until after the Second World War that this style of camera grew strongly in popularity. Most 35mm cameras at this time were of the

The Kine Exakta was used a lot by American submarine commanders.

rangefinder type, in which the viewfinder was separate from the lens and therefore did not see exactly the view that was recorded on film. If an exact preview of the picture being taken was needed, then a single lens reflex was required – and at the outbreak of the Second World War, the only known camera that fulfilled that need on 35mm film was the Kine Exakta. All of this explains why the Kine Exakta became a favourite with American submarine commanders, who recognised that the reflex system it employed made it easy to shoot pictures with the camera attached to a periscope. Kine Exaktas were also used by German war correspondents for the production of propaganda pictures.

The Kardon
In America in 1941, with the US Signal Corps in need of a quality 35mm camera, the government took advantage of the Alien Property Custodian Act to seize control of the New York branch of the German Leitz company,

The Kardon, known as the American Leica.

instructing them to produce Leica IIIa cameras for American military use. The company didn't prove up to the task, so the project was taken over by Peter Kardon, a naturalised US citizen born in Russia. Utilising Leitz equipment, he set out to make an American Leica. That didn't work either because it transpired that Leicas were practically handbuilt, and what the American government wanted was mass production. So Kardon came up with a new version that would fulfil those needs, producing a version similar to the Leica IIIa, but using an American Ektar lens. The camera was named the Kardon after the man who designed it.

Technically the camera was a success, but the government contract for the cameras was cancelled in 1945 when the war ended. Kardon endeavoured to turn his camera into a civilian model, but competition from Japanese and German cameras that soon began to appear on the market relegated the Kardon to history.

Ensign Midget

Because of its small size and the ease with which it could be secreted in a tunic pocket, the Ensign Midget was popular among soldiers who often smuggled the cameras overseas for their own purposes. Ensign itself was

In its vertical orientaion, the Ensign Midget, popular with both soldiers and civilians.

also keen to promote the camera as the ideal companion for soldiers and civilians alike during the war years. (More details about this camera in the previous chapter.)

Box cameras

Photography and quality camera buying in the years that led up to the Second World War were prohibitively expensive for most. At a time when the average wage for a manager or clerk was only a little over £7 a week, a Leica II cost nearly £28 and a Leica III might command more than £40, while the cost of a Rolleiflex Automat topped £25. For those on a tighter budget, whether civilians or soldiers who risked taking cameras to war, there was the humble box camera, many of which could be bought new for under ten shillings (50p).

Its style had been around since the first Kodak in 1888, but most of those on sale by the 1930s were little more than variations on the Kodak No.2 Brownie, which began life in 1901. It was a style of camera that would endure right through the war, into the 1950s and beyond. As its name suggests, the camera took the form of a box, sometimes made of metal,

English-made box cameras that were still popular at the time of the war: Six-20 Brownie (left), made by Kodak in London, and Ensign 2¼B (right), made by Houghton in Walthamstow.

The Brownie Reflex, a better-than-average snapshot camera, one of which was reputed to have saved its owner from injury under fire.

often from stout cardboard, with a lens at one end and a roll of film at the other. The focus was usually fixed, as was the aperture, although some more sophisticated models offered a choice of a few apertures, rendered by providing a strip of metal behind the lens punched with holes of different sizes. Box cameras were made by a great many manufacturers. Some, made by names like Zeiss Ikon, were capable of top-quality results, but most gave only average image quality that was more than acceptable to the photographer on a budget.

The Brownie Reflex was a slightly more sophisticated variation on the box camera theme, using twin lenses – one for shooting, the other to serve an extra-bright viewfinder. One such camera, carried by an American artilleryman during the Second World War, was reputed to have stopped a piece of shrapnel that might otherwise have seriously injured the camera's owner.

Movie cameras

During the war, AFPU-trained cinematographers made short black and white films, which were shown back home in commercial cinemas. Among these was the famous film *Desert Victory*, considered by many to be the definitive record of Britain's first victory on land during the Second World War. To shoot films like this and others, the AFPU issued its cinematographers with movie cameras made by several manufacturers.

Newman and Sinclair
Perhaps the best was a camera made by the British Newman and Sinclair company. It was a large box-shaped camera but its aluminium body made it lighter than might be expected. With a double-spring clockwork motor it was capable of running 200 feet of 35mm film without the motor needing to be rewound. One drawback was that the film loading had to be performed in the dark, but with no darkrooms on hand in the field, cinematographers were issued with changing bags. These took the form of large, light-tight bags into which the camera and unopened film were placed. The photographer then pushed his arms through two sleeves, elasticised to keep them light tight, and carried out the intricate manoeuvre of film loading sight unseen.

The British Newman and Sinclair
movie camera.

DeVry

American DeVry movie cameras earned the nickname of lunchbox
cameras because of their shape. Made with brown metal bodies, they
offered interchangeable lenses for shooting subjects close to or far away.
Despite taking 35mm film, the DeVry models were relatively small,
easy to transport and they each held 100ft reels of film. They ran by
clockwork, but could also be hand-cranked with the insertion of a handle
into a socket on the side. DeVry Model A and Model B cameras were
issued by the AFPU.

The American Devry 35mm cine camera.

Eyemo

Also from America came the Bell and Howell Eyemo, another 35mm camera used a lot for newsreel photography. It took 100 feet of film, but the clockwork motor wasn't capable of sustaining shooting for the complete roll and had to be wound at least twice for each film loaded. Most Eyemo cameras were fitted with revolving turrets, each containing three lenses that could be quickly turned into position. The lenses, whose focal lengths covered 35mm, 50mm and 150mm, allowed shooting at standard, which took in a similar field of view to the human eye; wide-angle, which opened up the view to include more each side, top and bottom of the image; and telephoto, which brought far subjects closer.

The American Eyemo movie camera, made by Bell and Howell.

Vinten

The British Vinten Model K, also known as the Normandy camera, was designed for the AFPU. It was painted in camouflage green and it too used three lenses on a turret to shoot wide-angle, standard and telephoto views. The viewfinder was engraved with markings to approximate the three different views taken in by the lenses. It took 100ft or 200ft reels of film that could be daylight loaded and driven through the camera by clockwork, battery or mains electrical motors.

The Vinten Model K, made in Britain.

Cunningham Combat Camera Model C

The Cunningham Combat Camera was built by the American War Department in 1941 and named after its designer, Harry Cunningham. It was a movie camera used for shooting live combat, seeing action in the latter days of the Second World War, and later during conflicts in the Far East.

The camera took 35mm film. It had three lenses that rotated into position on a turret, which also had space for a fourth. It was not a reflex camera and would not have been accurate at close-focusing distances, though that would have been immaterial when shooting battle scenes. The viewfinder above the turret showed the angle of view for the 35mm wide-angle lens and was etched with a rectangle that showed the view taken with the 75mm standard lens. Raising a magnifier into position within the viewfinder gave the view for the 150mm telephoto lens. A longer focal length 250mm telephoto lens was also available to screw into the turret's fourth slot, although the viewfinder did not give an accurate

The Cunningham Combat Camera.

representation of this lens's field of view, and view finding was largely guesswork on the part of the operator. The film was loaded into 200ft magazines, which were slid into the body with each one containing its own film gate. It was run through the camera by an electric motor, driven by two 45-volt batteries in series to provide 90 volts with speeds of sixteen, twenty-four or thirty-two frames per second.

The Cunningham Combat Camera was designed to be used handheld with the help of a pistol grip and rifle stock built onto the back of the body, which gave it the appearance of a submachine gun. There were stories of those being photographed mistaking the camera for a real gun and returning fire with live bullets. A manual supplied with each camera gave details of how to destroy it if captured by the enemy. The use of axes, petrol, flamethrowers and grenades was suggested.

Postcards

Postcards, which had grown into something of a novelty during the First World War, were far more commonplace by the time of the Second World War. Photographic studios were prevalent. Where there were soldiers, there were photographers to take their pictures and turn them into postcards to send home. Take, as an example, Sierra Leone

A selection of pictures of West Africa, produced during the Second World War by the Lisk-Carew company based in Freetown.

in West Africa. Because it was part of the British Empire, the colony was automatically pulled into the conflict when Britain declared war on Germany, and British forces were maintained there throughout the war. It was a fearsome place to be stationed, with its threat of diseases that included malaria, blackwater fever, yellow fever, fungal infections like dhobi itch, and dysentery in all its many forms. Not for nothing did the region earn itself the epithet of *The White Man's Grave*.

Yet, even before the start of the Second World War, the region was home to a photographic business run by brothers Alphonso and Arthur Lisk-Carew. Established as early as 1905, the brothers advertised their business, based in Sierra Leone's capital Freetown, as photographers, importers of photographic materials, stationery, toys, fancy goods, etc. The business was still running when Second World War soldiers arrived in the region. Here, soldiers could buy professionally photographed postcards showing the beauty rather than the harshness of the area, as well as film for their own cameras that they used in their leisure time plus processing facilities to develop and print their pictures. The studio was also available to take photographs of the soldiers that could be turned into postcards to send home.

One of many American propaganda postcards produced to mock the enemy.

Second World War postcards also played a part in propaganda, especially in America, once that country had entered the war at the end of 1941. Some of the postcards from this era were drawn and painted by artists, others relied on trick photography, which involved crudely produced montages of different photographs cut out and pasted together before being re-photographed. Many of these images showed Adolph Hitler either with or without several of his cohorts. The humour was, at best, of the toilet variety and often depicting a dog urinating on the fuehrer or on aspects of his way of life.

On the home front

Almost immediately the Second World War began it affected photography on the home front. Photographic magazines that had hitherto regularly published details of the latest cameras suddenly stopped listing German equipment in their editorial pages, even though some advertisers still sold German cameras that they had in stock. Even so, the inability to read reviews or hear announcements of the latest German products resulted in a fast downturn in photographic dealers' businesses. British companies whose trade involved the distribution of German cameras similarly suffered. All had to begin looking at new ways of running their businesses in the changed conditions. Adjustment and adaptability became their watchwords.

Professional portrait photographers were not badly affected at first and, indeed, some even reported a mini boom in business. Technical and advertising photographers, however, saw their businesses slump. Press photographers were particularly affected since pictures of war, which were most in demand, were the very subjects that government restrictions prevented them from taking. In reaction they turned to shooting pictures of topical interest at home, using imagination and creativity to make what had previously been mundane more interesting for magazine and newspaper readers.

As manufactures and dealers strove to keep prices from rising, amateur photography was not initially affected too much. Military subjects were now taboo, but it was suggested that because war broke out at the end of the year, these were less likely to be the kinds of subjects tackled by amateurs

Dallmeyer lenses compare themselves to the British navy in a 1941 advertisement.

in the winter months anyway. That said, the photographic trade's profits were not helped by the fact that many amateur photographers, who had been the trade's bread and butter, were no longer practising photography, having been called away to fight in the war.

It wasn't long after the outbreak of war that manufacturers began to feel its effects. In a 1940 advertisement (which would have been prepared for press at the end 1939), the British camera manufacturer Soho announced...

Owing to heavy National demands on our factories, we are unable to supply the full requirements of many of our customers.

Not that the company seemed too despondent about the situation, as the advertisement continued, in a way that seemed to contradict its first statement...

The war period with its great upheavals will present new opportunities for many. Be sure that you do not miss them. Remember that we are in a position to supply every requirement of the professional photographer, including frames, mounts and general photographic sundries, and most of these are actually in stock.

Other manufactures were swift to jump on the wartime bandwagon in an effort to sell goods. The British Fallowfield company, which sold a wide range of photographic sundries, announced that it had eighty years of experience in the trade: '1856 – 1940: Crimean to Hitler's war'. A later advertisement from the same company listed its associations with several wars:

Crimean War: Fallowfields started with photography.
Boer War: Fallowfields supplied all X-Ray plates.
Great War: Hospitals and Government supplies.
Hitler's War: We are still supplying and helping.

At the same time, patriotic pictures began appearing in photographic companies' advertisements: flag waving and battleships on the high seas to attract readers to Johnson's British chemicals; a soldier in his tin helmet to advertise the Ensign Ful-Vue camera; more battleships and flags to sell British Dallmeyer and Cooke lenses; aircraft in air-to-air combat to remind everyone that 'when the battle flags are finally furled, Gebescope projectors will again be available for civilian use'.

Portfolios of readers' photographs that regularly appeared in photographic magazines now began to take a new turn. Pages that had previously been dominated by photographs of gentle landscapes, cute babies, portraits, character studies and nudes now included powerful pictures of soldiers in uniform and abstract interpretations of war. Taylor Hobson, who made Cooke lenses, summed it up in a 1944 advertisement...

Today, British Cooke lenses are focused on new subjects: the pastoral scene has become a battlefield, the court gown a uniform. The times have altered, the scene has changed, but Cooke lenses remain the first choice of serious photographers.

Bell and Howell looks forward to a brighter future in a 1941 advertisement.

Yet some photographic companies tried their very best to be optimistic. Illustrated by a picture of a mother and child at the top of a hill, watching the sun rise over a tranquil landscape, the Bell and Howell company, which specialised in amateur cine cameras and projectors, announced...

Optimism or, if you like, hope, is the eternal incentive for carrying on. The hope of better things to come is the soldier's best weapon on the battlefield, it is the sailor's final port and the compass where the airman guides his aircraft back to safe and ultimate landing. With all the word at war, the nation's brains and brawn are stretched to the limit in the production of apparatus for destruction, but the time will come, and may well be nearer than we anticipate, when the peaceful pursuits of the arts, learning and commerce will again occupy men's minds.

Soft-centred optimism certainly seemed to be the keyword in Bell and Howell's philosophy. To quote a 1943 advertisement from the company...

When the rifles and tin hats are laid aside; when Hitler, Bock and Rommel have disappeared from the headlines; when Piccadilly Circus glitters again and friendly lights twinkle in English hamlets – Bell and Howell will again be able to pursue their policy of providing the best professional and amateur cinematographic equipment.

There were, however, places where the war actually helped photographic progress. As the editorial in the 1943 *British Journal Photographic Almanac* pointed out...

The war has given tremendous impetus to discovery and invention in photography as in all else, although at the moment the results are largely hidden in the interests of national security. Not only have many new materials and processes been evolved, but many weaknesses have been revealed, including shortages of raw, intermediate and finished products which never should have occurred. One advantage which has resulted is the enforcing of a more economical utilisation of materials not only as regards quantity, but also with a view to obtaining the best possible result of which the material is capable.

War reparations

Germany's defeat in the Second World War led to major disruptions and significant changes for two of the country's largest camera manufacturers. They were Ernst Leitz, makers of Leica cameras, and Zeiss Ikon, makers of Contax cameras.

Leica copies

Following the war, camera manufacturers from around the world began copying and faking Germany's Leica cameras. The models that were most copied and faked were: the 1932 Leica II, a 35mm camera with a coupled rangefinder; and the 1933 Leica III, which added an extra dial to provide slow shutter speeds and went on to introduce a series of subtle variations – IIIa, IIIb, IIIc, IIId, IIIf and IIIg (but no IIIe) – well into the 1950s. The practice of copying these cameras was perfectly legal for two reasons.

Firstly, when Leica cameras were originally made, Leitz failed to register patents in Russia or China. As a result, the Russians began making copies of the Leica II as early as 1934, two years after the introduction of the real thing. Production was interrupted by the outbreak of war, but continued when the war ended with a great many of these Russian cameras produced under the names Fed, made by a company of the same name in the Ukraine, and Zorki, made by the Krasnogorsk Mechanical Factory near Moscow.

The second reason why Leicas were legally copied so freely lay in the fact that with the end of the war, governments of countries in which

Russian Fed (left) and Zorki (right) cameras, both copies of the Leica II.

The Reid III, a copy of the Leica IIIb.

German patents had been registered made those patents available free of charge to the public and industry. Consequently, post-war, camera manufacturers all over the world began making their own versions of Leica cameras. Most copies were based on the Leica II or Leica III. Among them were: the Reid III, a copy of the Leica IIIb made in 1947 by the British firm Reid and Sigrist; and the Canon SII, a copy of the Leica III also made in 1947 by the Canon Camera Company in Japan. Both of these companies made further variations on the original models, and alongside these British and Japanese manufacturers, a huge plethora of Leica copies were also made in countries that included France, Germany, Italy and America.

Leica fakes

While Leica copies have no pretence of being anything other than cameras that have been copied from, or which have been strongly influenced by, original Leicas, fakes were a different matter. Faking Leicas began soon after the war and continues to this day. Most of these fakes began life as Fed or Zorki cameras, but instead of bearing those names as was the case with legitimate copies, they were engraved with 'Leica' on the bodies and 'Elmar' (the lens name most associated with the cameras that they emulated) on the lenses.

Many of these cameras really do look like the real thing, although a true Leica aficionado will soon spot the difference through the general feel and operation of the camera, while serial numbers are not consistent with the real thing. Others are very obviously fakes, with snakeskin or faux wooden bodies and gold fittings never found on the real cameras. Some of these claim references to the Second World War. One example of this fakery is a Leica II copy with a gold lamé body and fake gold fittings, which claims to have been made for the Luftwaffe and goes so far as engraving a German eagle clutching a swastika in its claws on the camera body and lens cap. Another example, again a Leica II copy, has a fake wooden body, gold fittings and engravings on the body and lens cap referring to the *King George V* battleship and the date 11 December 1940, the date the ship was commissioned.

Although cameras like these have associations with the Second World War and what happened to Leica cameras in its aftermath, few if any date back to those immediately post-war days and are still being made today purely for the collector's market.

A camera that claims to have been made for the German Luftwaffe and is engraved with a swastika on its top and lens cap is actually a post-war fake.

Contax copies

Contax II and III cameras were made at the Zeiss Ikon works in Dresden in 1936. Production of both ceased in 1941 and, towards the end of the war in February 1945, the Zeiss factory was damaged in an Allied bombing raid, leaving it impossible for camera production to continue.

As the war ended, Dresden fell into the Russian zone of East Germany. According to the terms of the peace agreement, Germany had to pay war reparation to the victors and among the many German products that the Russians wanted were the Contax II and III cameras. Following the destruction of most of Zeiss Ikon's records during the firebombing of Dresden in 1945, the Russians demanded complete sets of drawings for the cameras to be recreated. They also required the machinery needed to make the cameras, training and installation information, sample cameras and accessories. With this, the Russians set up their own production lines to start building trial cameras again in Germany, still under the Zeiss name.

When it was ascertained that the cameras could be successfully produced, the entire factory, including its wooden internal walls and toilets, was shifted to Kiev, where deported Zeiss personnel trained Russian workers in the complexities of camera manufacture. The cameras that resulted from this operation were direct copies of the Contax models, but bore the name Kiev, after the town in Ukraine in which they were built. Over the following years, minor modification to the original Zeiss concepts resulted in new styles of Kiev, including a copy of the Contax III with its built-in exposure meter. The cameras continued to be

The Russian Kiev camera (left) with the German Contax II (right) from which it was copied.

modified and improved upon right through to the 1970s, but at the hearts of them all lay the pre-war Contax cameras from Zeiss Ikon.

At the same time, in Stuttgart, which lay in the American Zone of Germany following the war, and with the encouragement of the Americans, plans were afoot to resurrect the original Contax II and III cameras. The only factory available for the process was one run by Contessa-Nettel, which had been absorbed into Zeiss Ikon along with other German camera manufacturers back in 1926. With no plans readily available, the engineers involved had only samples of the original Contax cameras to work with. They were stripped down, examined and new plans drawn up. From these, two new cameras rose from the ashes of their predecessors. They appeared in 1950 under the names Contax IIa and IIIa. While of similar design to their predecessors, these new cameras incorporated improvements that gave them a slightly smaller size and more reliability. Today they are still considered top-class classic cameras.

Meanwhile in Japan, the Allied occupying force that took command at the end of the war turned its attention to optical instrument maker Nippon Kogaku, first allowing the company to resume production of

The Contax IIIa produced in West Germany following the war.

telescopes and microscopes, and then to begin thinking about building a camera. The result was the first of one of photography's most famous names and an illustrious line of cameras that continues today. The camera was the Nikon I, whose design owed something to both Zeiss and Leitz in Germany. Outwardly, the Nikon I strongly resembled a Contax II and even used the same lens mount. Internally, it owed more to the workings of the Leica IIIa. In the years ahead, that first Contax-like camera evolved into new models that included the Nikon M, Nikon S and Nikon SP.

So, within a few years of the end of the Second World War, and as a direct consequence of that war, a new kind of 35mm camera, heavily influenced by the Leica, began to appear around the world, while at the same time there existed four versions of the Contax II and III cameras: the originals that had survived from before the war; the Kiev copies that were slightly inferior; the much improved Contax IIa and IIIa; and the first Nikons.

This last range of Japanese cameras in particular marked the beginning of the decline of Germany as a world-beating camera manufacturing country and the start of Japan's rise to prominence in a field that, within a few years, it would dominate.

Chapter 10

Focus On: The Kodak Medalist

If ever a camera *looked* like it should be a military model, it was the Medalist. Built by Kodak in America and introduced in 1941, the camera was nothing like the company had ever made before and, with the exception of a second similar model introduced after the war, nothing like it would ever build again. The Medalist was big, heavy, remarkably rugged, and looked like it might be indestructible. It measured $13 \times 11 \times 11$cm, weighed 1.5 kilos and shot eight big 6×9cm

First model of the Kodak Medalist, a rugged American camera from 1941.

images to a roll of film, which ensured better quality than images from a 35mm camera. It was issued to troops the year America entered the war and used primarily for colour photography.

Kodak's annual catalogue for 1941 was issued in February that year. On 7 December, the Japanese attacked Pearl Harbor, one of the factors that led to America being drawn into the Second World War. As a consequence, there was no full size catalogue for 1942. Instead, Kodak issued an insert to the 1941 catalogue whose main feature was the introduction of the Medalist, which was described in this way...

A radical departure in camera design, the Kodak Medalist is also a photographic instrument of remarkable ability and fineness. In one compact assembly it combines the convenience of roll film with easy adaptability to ground-glass focusing, back extensions and the negative material range of a view camera... and adds the scope, accuracy and operating refinements of a precision miniature. This has never before been accomplished in any known camera of this type.

The designers

By the end of the 1930s, Kodak had a special department to manage the complexities of camera design, handled by mechanical designers and exterior body stylists. Those associated with the Medalist are likely to have been Joseph Mihalyi for the camera's mechanics, with the exterior styling conceived by Walter Dorwin Teague. Both designers had excellent pedigrees.

Mihalyi was a Hungarian who came to America in 1907 where he was hired by Kodak in 1923 as an apparatus designer. Teague was an industrial designer whose design company won a contract with Kodak in 1927. Both men were named on the Medalist patents. In a patent dated 11 February 1941, it is Mihalyi who speaks about a new type of roll film camera 'so designed that improper operation of the various parts thereof is prevented'. Mihalyi and Teague were both named on a following patent of 28 October 1941, in which they jointly stated that they had invented 'a new, original and ornamental design for cameras'.

Using a Medalist

Bearing in mind that the camera troops might have been using before the issue of the Medalist was a Speed Graphic, with all the complications of a glass plate camera, using the new camera should have been a lot simpler. In many ways, however, it was even more complicated.

Before loading with film, a small exposure counter window on the top plate needed to be checked to make sure the number '0' appeared in it. If any other number was apparent, a knob beside the window was turned to bring the '0' into position. If this wasn't done, then the winding mechanism would jam up as the film was loaded. Twin latches on each side of the camera back both took the form of two pins slotted into tiny tubular sockets top and bottom of the body. In this way, the latches also acted as hinges. Consequently, the back could be opened from the left, or from the right, or removed entirely.

The Medalist used 620 size roll film, which was similar to the more traditional 120 size but rolled onto thinner spindles to make the roll more compact and so reduce the size of the camera, although in the case of the bulky body of the Medalist, any reduction was not noticeable. The film was slotted into the empty chamber on the right of the body, where a sprung roller held it firmly in place. It was then led over a second roller, across the film plane and over a third roller before being attached to the

The back of the camera could be opened from either side.

Top plate of the camera showing the film wind knob, film type reminder, exposure counter, focusing scale and shutter release.

take-up spool. When the back was closed, a fourth roller, in the camera's back, pressed against roller number three, sandwiching the film tightly between them. Small spikes top and bottom of the third roller ensured that the film was firmly gripped. The reason for this was that as the film was wound, its tightness and attachment to the third roller was secure enough to turn it and so tension the shutter.

With the back closed, the film was wound until '1' appeared in the red window, whereupon the exposure counter on the top plate was also set at '1'. From there on, the exposure counter could be used to count off the eight exposures, without reference to the red window. That is, unless the photographer was using Kodacolor, the most popular colour film of the day. With that film loaded, the photographer had to think differently. Kodacolor in 620 size at that time was supplied in six-exposure rolls with an extra length of film at the end of each roll. This was used as a processing control, and wasn't designed to be exposed in the camera. Kodacolor users loaded up in much the same way, but when '1' was seen in the red window, the exposure counter on top of the body needed to be set to '3'. From then on, the exposure counter was always two numbers ahead of the actual exposure: '3' in the exposure counter equating to '1' in the red window through to '8' in the exposure counter equating to '6' in the red window. In case a photographer forgot what type of film was loaded, or how which number indicated what exposure, there was a dial on the left of the top plate that could be turned against an index mark to indicate the film in use.

Opposite this film type dial stood another dial that indicated focusing distances. A depth of field scale sat in the middle of this. To focus the lens, a large ring around its edge was turned causing the lens to begin moving outwards from the body on a helical screw. When it reached its infinity setting, the dial on the top kicked into action and, from then on, it rotated as the lens was wound out further to indicate focusing distances down to 3.5 feet. Fine focusing was possible by use of a knob below and to the side of the lens.

The viewfinder was mounted above the rangefinder and engraved with the camera name. Looking through the viewfinder showed a large window with a smaller one beneath. The larger window was the actual viewfinder. The smaller one was a split-image rangefinder coupled to the focusing.

The lens was a Kodak Ektar with apertures set on a ring around its edge and indicated on a scale at the top of the lens barrel from f/3.5 to f/32. The shutter was a Kodak Supermatic No.2 with speeds from 1 second to 1/400 second plus 'B' indicated on another scale behind the aperture settings. The scale was divided into two halves for slow speeds and high speeds. 1, 1/2, 1/5 and 1/10 second were shown on the left, then there was a gap and 1/25, 1/50, 1/100, 1/200 and 1/400 second were shown on the right. This necessitated twin pointers spaced a little way apart on the setting ring: a red one to line up against the slow speeds and a black one to line up against the fast speeds. Both shutter speeds and apertures could be read from the top of the camera for easy adjustment.

The shutter release was on the right of the body, surrounded by a locking lever. Once the exposure had been made, the film was wound, automatically tensioning the shutter for the next shot. As each exposure was made, a red signal appeared in a small window behind the focusing scale, disappearing as the film was wound and reappearing once the subsequent exposure had been made. Double exposures were permissible by tensioning the shutter manually by means of a lever bedside the viewfinder. A ten-second self timer was activated by a lever to the side of the lens.

The accessories

To make the camera more versatile, a range of accessories was available. Chief among these was the Kodak Accessory Back for sheet film, film packs and plates. It took the form of a replacement back, which fitted onto the camera in the same way as the normal back. The difference was that, under a focusing hood that unfolded from the rear there was a ground-glass screen used for focusing. As the Accessory Back was clicked into place, a small lug on its inside surface automatically adjusted the

The camera with its accessory back and hooded focusing screen fitted.

rangefinder, focusing scale and viewfinder parallax to account for the difference between the roll film plane and the sheet film/plate plane.

The screen and its hood were hinged so that they could be swung aside, or they could be detached completely to allow holders for sheet film or plates to be slid into position. These were of the traditional type that held a dark slide to be pulled away for the exposure to be made, and then slid back into position before the holder was removed. A film pack holder could also be slotted into position in a similar way.

Before the Accessory Back could be put into action for plates, cut film or film packs, it needed to be adjusted for the specific camera to which it was attached. To do this, the lens was first fully retracted. Then the Accessory Back was fitted to the camera and the ground-glass panel and hood removed to reveal four screws, one in each corner of the Back. These were loosened to create a slight clearance between the inner corner of a spacer frame and the camera back frame. A piece of paper was then slipped into the space at one of the corners and the screw at that corner

With the focusing screen swung aside and a sheet film holder slid into place; the film pack back is seen in front.

The camera with the spacer and focusing screen hood assembled.

carefully tightened until the paper was in contact with the spacer frame and the camera back. When it was in its correct position it took a very slight effort to remove the paper. If the paper tore, the adjustment was too tight and the screw had to be loosened off a little. That corner was then correctly adjusted, and the procedure was repeated on the other three corners. In this way, the Accessory Back was adjusted for that particular Medalist camera. It could not be used on any other camera without being adjusted again.

On any camera, getting the lens to focus nearer than the normal close focusing distance necessitates fitting close-up lenses, or increasing the distance between lens and film or plate. The Medalist could be fitted with any of three Kodak Portra close-up lenses, the strongest of which allowed focusing down to 10 inches, to cover a subject of $5\frac{1}{4} \times 7\frac{1}{2}$ inches.

To increase the distance between the lens and film or plate, the Medalist did things in an unusual way. The lens of course was fixed, and so could not be extended from the body on bellows or tubes as would be the case with an interchangeable lens camera. Instead, the focusing screen and hood were removed from the Accessory Back, which was then attached to the camera in the normal way. A Spacer accessory was then fitted to

Filters and lens hood available for the Medalist.

the Accessory Back and the focusing screen and hood refitted to the end of the Spacer. This had the effect of increasing the distance between the lens and film or plate, so allowing closer focusing. It was possible to fit several spacers to each other for even closer focusing. Alternatively, with four spacers fitted and the addition of the Kodak Telek lens to the front of the cameras lens, telephoto effects could be achieved.

Filters were also available for the camera, but they didn't screw into the lens mount as might be expected. Instead, they were dropped into the lens mount on the front of the lens and held in place by a special retaining ring that screwed into the mount. They could also be held in place by the lens hood, which also screwed into the mount. Filters available included a skylight; polariser; three strengths of yellow, green and red; plus infra-red.

The Medalist I was not synchronised for flash. So if a flashgun was to be used it needed to be in conjunction with a synchroniser. This was an accessory that screwed into the cable release socket and to which the flashgun was wired. As a lever was pressed to trip the shutter, the synchroniser also made the electrical contact required to fire the flash.

The Medalist in popular culture

The extent to which the Medalist caught the imagination of the public and entered popular culture is nicely illustrated by its appearance on the cover of a popular American comic book of the time. *Camera Comics* ran for nine issues from October 1944 to June 1946. Each edition featured cartoon characters who used cameras: Kid Click; Linda Lens; and The Grey Comet, Army Air Force Photographer of the Air. It also contained fact-based stories about photographic pioneers such as George Eastman, the founder of Kodak.

In issue 3 of *Camera Comics*, published in December 1944, Linda Lens, woman photographer, fights the Germans and is depicted on the cover delivering a nasty blow to one of them with her Medalist, swung on the end of its strap.

Linda Lens uses her Medalist to thwart the enemy on the cover of a 1944 issue of *Camera Comics*.

Chapter 11

The Cold War

Although America and Russia fought on the same side during the Second World War, the two countries were very far from being true allies. Throughout the war each treated the other with distrust. When the war ended, both went their separate ways, and a Cold War developed. It was not a war in which military forces physically fought one another in battle, but one in which each nation fought stealthily for its own beliefs: American capitalism versus Russian communism. The

Aerial photography was still important in the Cold War, using updates of cameras developed during the Second World War. This is a Konica Aerial Type G camera from the mid-1960s.

Cold War began as the Second World War ended in 1945 and continued until the dissolution of the Soviet Union at the end of 1991.

During these years, espionage was rife on both sides, leading to new needs for equipment to assist spying. As a result, two types of camera were called into service. First, there were those that had been launched before the Second World War, but whose attributes now made them suitable for covert photography. Alongside these came more specialised cameras whose designs made them suitable for incorporation into some other everyday object that allowed them to be used clandestinely.

As an aside, it is interesting to note the part played by collectors in the development of certain cameras that originated in this era. A great many Russian cameras, including those used for espionage purposes, were largely unknown outside the Soviet Union until the time of its dissolution. As the country began to open up, however, cameras that no one in the West had seen before came to light, and they were soon sought out and purchased by collectors. Recognising a market for such cameras, small engineering businesses, mostly in Poland, began making them purely for collectors. Some of these were direct copies of cameras that had genuinely been used for espionage purposes; others were new designs dreamt up by enterprising engineers purely for the collectors' market. As a result, so-called spy cameras emerged, many of which had

The Ticka, a camera that looks like a pocket watch, might appear to have been manufactured for Cold War espionage, but it was actually made as far back as 1905, when there was a craze for disguised cameras.

little true connection with spying, and some of which were actually made in the years after the Cold War ended.

It is also worth understanding that cameras disguised as other everyday objects actually date back to as early as 1862 when Thompson's Revolver camera was made in France, and other disguised cameras continued to be made right up until the digital age. Objects known to have concealed cameras, during this time, included books, cravats, walking sticks, waistcoat buttons, tiepins, parcels, belts, rings, lighters, matchboxes, cigarette packets, pocket watches, wristwatches, pens, hats, handbags, powder compacts, briefcases, binoculars, radios and even guns. Many of these were designed for use by photographers who enjoyed taking candid pictures without being noticed by the people they were photographing, or for no reason other than the fact that the camera-buying pubic developed crazes every so often for disguised models. Such cameras were made for everyday use, rather than for true espionage purposes.

Existing cameras

Although some cameras were made, or adapted, to satisfy the needs of Cold War espionage, there were other already existing cameras that had been around since before the Second World War and which were now called into service for spying purposes. Here are some of the more notable.

Minox subminiature

Of all the spy cameras ever made, the Minox is probably the best known – mainly because it was never intended to be a spy camera in the first place. Its inventor saw it only as a precision subminiature camera with a reliable shutter and an excellent lens for consumer use. First made in Latvia in 1937, production was interrupted by the outbreak of the Second World War in 1939 when Latvia was occupied first by the Russians, followed by the Germans, then by the Russians again. Limited production of the Minox continued during these turbulent times, but when the war ended in 1945, production of a new generation of cameras resumed in West Germany. It was this second generation of Minoxes that found its way into the hands of Cold War photographers for both conventional

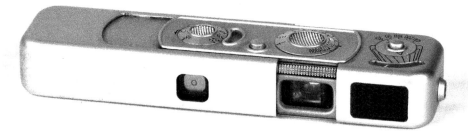

The Minox B, the most popular post-war Minox camera.

purposes and document photography. (More about this fascinating little camera in the next chapter.)

Leica

First launched in 1925, the Leica was used during the Second World War by war correspondents and the military on both sides of the conflict: the Allies using cameras that were already in the country at the outbreak of war, the Germans with cameras made by Leitz especially for their use. They included cameras like the Leica IIIc, some of which were made by Leitz specially engraved for the Wehrmacht, Germany's armed forces.

A specially adapted lens cap allows a Leica to be used with the cap seeming to cover the lens.

Traditionally, Leica cameras used lens caps to protect their lenses when not in use, engraved with the Leica name. For espionage purposes, special lens caps were made with the Leica name cut out. In its traditional position, with the dark lens behind it, the name looked like a black logo. It was possible, however, for the lens to shoot images through the cut-out name. In this way, pictures could be taken while, to all outward appearances, the camera's lens cap was in place.

Tessina

Made by the Swiss firm Concava in 1961, the Tessina was another camera that was not originally intended for espionage purposes but found itself recruited for the purpose, not least because it could be worn on the wrist like a watch and concealed by the user's sleeve.

At $65 \times 50 \times 20$mm, the Tessina was about the size and shape of a matchbox, with two lenses on the side where, if it were a matchbox, the match would be struck. Inside, two mirrors were used, one to reflect light from the main lens down to the film, which ran at right angles to it, the other to reflect light from a second lens up to a viewing screen on top of the flat body. The camera incorporated a clockwork motor drive to advance the film.

The Tessina on its wrist strap, enabling it to be worn like a watch.

As well as their use on the wrist, Tessina cameras were also known to be hidden inside items such as cigarette packets. In this incarnation, the camera was held in place by a harness inside the packet so that its lens was aligned with a small hole in the exterior. The shutter release could be pressed through the flexible pack and the camera was capable of shooting ten pictures before the clockwork motor drive needed to be rewound.

There is also evidence of Tessina cameras being hidden in recesses cut out of the pages of books with the lens lined up with an aperture that appeared to be one of a series of index markers printed on the edges of all the pages.

Steineck ABC

Made in 1948, the Steineck ABC was an American camera produced more for lovers of novelty cameras than for genuine espionage purposes. It couldn't be described as a disguised camera because, although worn on the wrist like a watch, it had no watch face and made no pretence to be anything other than a camera. Even so, at first glance, it could be mistaken for a wristwatch and was easily hidden under a sleeve.

Resembling a wristwatch, the Steineck ABC was sometimes called into service for espionage purposes.

The camera was a precision instrument, even though specification was meagre: a tiny Steinheil 12.5mm f/2.5 lens at the 12 o'clock position on the 'watch face' and a single speed shutter. It took eight circular exposures, each one 5.5mm on a disc of film, cut from normal 35mm film using a special punch supplied with the camera. As each exposure was made, the disc rotated to the next position for the following exposure. At the time of its launch, clip-on filters, close-up lenses and even a miniature enlarger were available.

With such a small size of image the camera would not have been capable of producing the kind of quality obtainable from 35mm film, or even the 16mm film used by many spy cameras. For all these reasons, although the camera might have occasionally been called into service, it is unlikely to have been used extensively for espionage purposes.

Minox 35mm

In 1974, after thirty-seven years of making subminiature cameras, Minox switched to ultra-small 35mm models. The Minox 35EL was the first and it won its own place in the world of espionage. Advertised to consumers

The Minox EL was easily concealed and useful for document photography.

as the world's smallest full-frame 35mm camera, it was tiny, measuring no more than a pocket-size $9.5 \times 6 \times 2.5$cm when folded. Unfolding a flap from the front allowed the lens to come forward into its shooting position. Focus was manual but a built-in meter offered aperture-priority automatic exposure.

The small size of the camera, an excellently sharp lens, ease of use and the fact that it took standard 35mm film made it ideal for clandestine and document photography. Its only drawback was its reliance on a battery for operation. Such was its popularity in the West, however, that a Soviet Union camera manufacturer made its own exact copy, calling it the Kiev 35A.

Pentax Auto 110

In 1972, Kodak introduced a new type of film called 110. It was actually 16mm film stored in twin cassettes, which, when inserted into the camera, wound from one chamber to the other. The film's primary and most popular use was in basic snapshot cameras, made by a great many manufacturers around the world. Two Japanese companies, however, made more sophisticated single lens reflexes to take 110 film. They were Minolta and Pentax and, of the two, it was the Pentax cameras that were taken up by Russian Cold War photographers.

The Pentax Auto 110 was launched in 1979. It resembled a conventional 35mm camera reduced to just $9 \times 5 \times 3$cm. Despite its miniature size, this was a fully functioning singe lens reflex with an impressive range of

The Pentax Auto 110, with its range of interchangeable lenses.

interchangeable lenses. The standard lens had a focal length of 24mm, which gave a similar field of view to a standard 50mm lens on a 35mm camera. Also available were an 18mm wide-angle, 50mm and 70mm telephotos, and a 20–40mm zoom. The camera stood at the centre of a system of accessories that included a flashgun, motor drive, filters and close-up lenses.

Exposure was automatic with green and yellow light emitting diodes (LEDs) in the viewfinder. Green indicated a shutter speed of above 1/45 second had been selected by the camera, which meant it could be handheld; yellow warned of camera shake because the speed had fallen to below 1/45 second. If that was the case, the camera was equipped for tripod mounting. Film was wound by a lever that required two strokes. In 1982, the camera was upgraded as the Pentax Auto 110 Super, which added a larger viewfinder, a delayed action feature and one-stroke film advance.

Although these cameras were small enough to be hidden in the palm of the hand and therefore easy to use secretly, they were more often employed for document photography.

Cameras for concealment

If a spy camera was to be concealed inside some other object it needed to be small and easy to manipulate sight-unseen. One German and two Russian cameras fulfilled those needs admirably and subsequently found their way into all kinds of objects from handbags to attaché cases, from cigarette packets to umbrellas and more.

Robot

When an operative was using a concealed camera, and knew certain conditions under which a picture needed to be taken, it was possible to adjust apertures and shutter speeds in advance for correct exposure. Likewise the lens could be pre-focused. The difficulty lay in winding the film after each exposure, especially if several shots needed to be taken quickly and consecutively. That problem was solved by use of cameras with clockwork motor drives that could be tensioned in advance to automatically wind the film as soon as each exposure had been made. The Robot camera was one of two obvious choices for the job.

The Robot Star was a clockwork motor drive camera current at the time of the Cold War.

By the time of the Cold War, German-made Robot cameras that were first seen in the 1930s had evolved and the latest model was the Robot Star. Like its predecessors, the camera incorporated a clockwork motor, wound by a large knob on the top of the body, which automatically advanced the film after each exposure. The camera took 35mm film in standard cassettes of the day and shot 24 × 24mm square pictures, fifty to each roll of film. Later, in 1969, new versions of the camera were produced with a change in body style and more powerful motor drives. The Star 25 was capable of shooting twenty-five pictures in succession without rewinding the motor; the Star 50 could shoot fifty exposures with just one wind of the motor. The cameras had interchangeable lenses that covered wide-angle, standard and telephoto focal lengths.

It was of course the clockwork film advance that made Robot cameras so useful for espionage purposes. Aware of how their cameras could be put to use in the espionage world, the manufacturers made a range of accessories that aided their use for covert photography. The camera was used by spies in both the East and the West.

F-21 / Ajax-12

The F-21 was the second, and probably more popular, choice of camera with a clockwork-driven film advance. Its style was strongly influenced by the Robot, but it was much smaller, measuring only 7 × 5 × 4.5cm. Like the Robot, it had a winding knob on top of the body, which gave up to ten exposures to each wind. Shutter speeds of 1/10-1/100 second were set by a lever on the top plate, while apertures from f/2 to f/16 were set on a ring around the lens, which focused down to 2 metres.

The F-21, originally called the Ajax-12, was first made in 1951 by Krasnogorsk Mekanicheski Zavod (Krasnogorsk Mechanical Factory). Its origins are thought to lie with a similar camera, without a motor drive, from an unknown Russian maker possibly based in Ufa, the capital of the Republic of Bachkaria. Called the M-F, this is thought to have been made for the Russian secret service in 1950 and led to a clockwork motor-

The F-21, styled like a miniature Robot camera.

driven version called the MF-1. It was this that Krasnogorsk adopted and turned into the F-21. The two cameras were very similar, except for a slightly different top plate and rounded ends on the F-21, compared to squarer ends on the MF-1. Both the motor drive and the shutter were whisper quiet, which, coupled with the automatic film advance, made it the ideal camera for concealment in other objects when used for covert photography. The camera could be fitted into a harness secreted inside the appropriate object for its disguise. The harness incorporated a cable that fitted over the camera's shutter release at one end and a firing mechanism at the other end, suitable for concealment in a pocket.

The camera took 35mm film and produced a half-frame image of 18×21mm. However, it was too small to take standard 35mm cassettes. Instead, 35mm film was cut down to a 21mm width, using a special film splitter, which removed the sprocket holes and loaded into a feed cassette, linked to the take-up cassette by a metal bridge. It was recommended to use a special film with an ultra-thin emulsion, and a length of around 60cm gave enough for eighteen exposures.

Ajax versions of the camera were made in several styles, including the Ajax-8 in which the clockwork motor drive was replaced by a plunger that could be depressed by the thumb to wind the film. It made the camera smaller and more easily concealed in the palm of the hand.

The F-21 had an especially long life with versions still being made as late as 1994, although in the latter years it is more likely that the cameras were made for collectors, rather than for genuine spying purposes.

Kiev-30

Sixteen millimetre film, which was first used in a still camera called the Mini-Fex in 1932, lay dormant throughout the Second World War, then rose to popularity again in the 1950s, when it began to be used in every type of camera from single lens reflexes to twin lens reflexes, from stereo to panoramic models and more. For a while it seemed the format would take over from 35mm as the most popular film type, but then, in the 1960s, its use mostly waned and died. In Ukraine, however, at the Arsenal factory in Kiev, 16mm cameras continued to be made in the 1960s and on into the 1970s, with designs similar to Japanese Minolta 16 cameras from the 1950s.

Kiev 30M, a Russian subminiature camera that was easily concealed for espionage purposes.

The Kiev 30 incorporated into a fingerprint copying device.

The Kiev 30, first made in 1974, is the one most associated with concealment. It took the shape of a small, flat box measuring $8 \times 4.5 \times 2.5$cm in its closed position, but whose length increased from 8cm to 11cm when one end was pulled out like a drawer for shooting the picture. Doing so unmasked the lens and viewfinder, while revealing the shutter release and a thumbwheel used for focusing the lens. Apertures from f/3.5-f/11 and shutter speeds of 1/30-1/200 second were set on thumbwheels on one end of the camera.

The Kiev-30 and a simplified successor called the Kiev-30M were incorporated into fingerprint copying devices, as well as objects such as fake cigarette packets for covert photography.

Spy cameras

Until its breakup in 1991, the Russian KGB, whose name in English translates as the Committee for State Security, was a military-style organisation responsible for internal security, the collection of foreign intelligence and the secret police. In America, the Central Intelligence Agency (CIA) was, and still is, a civilian part of the federal government that gathers, processes and analyses national security information worldwide. During the Cold War, both sides employed cameras for espionage, some

The harness with fake button that housed an F-21 or Ajax 12 camera and its attached shutter release control.

A set of different types of button that could be interchanged for concealed shooting.

of which were used in plain sight, and a great many of which were used concealed inside some other everyday object.

The F-21 or Ajax 12 cameras were particularly popular for concealment, especially in clothing, where the lens shot pictures through fake buttons while the shutter was released by an attached control hidden in a pocket.

Man's attaché case

To all outward appearances, this was a flat case of the type carried by businessmen the world over; inside it held a complicated harness that was built to accept a Russian Zola Spy Camera, which was modified from another Russian camera called the Zorki 6.

The Zorki 6, built from 1948 to 1978, was an ordinary 35mm rangefinder model made for the consumer market. To convert it into a Zola, the lens was removed and the opening that would normally allow the lens's light to reach the film was blocked off. The viewfinder and light meter built into the original camera were removed and replaced with a small lens that now stood at right angles to the film. A prism system then reflected light from the lens to the film. A clockwork motor drive was also incorporated to wind the film.

The original Zorki 6 camera.

How the Zorki was adapted for use in the briefcase.

The harness inside the case that held the camera.

The camera in its harness.

With the camera inserted into the attaché case's harness, the lens was positioned to shoot through a small opening in the end of the case. The shutter was released by a switch on the handle of the case and was linked electronically to the camera's normal shutter release. After exposure, the clockwork motor advanced the film ready for the next shot.

The innocent-looking case that was nevertheless equipped and ready for clandestine photography.

A similar briefcase was used by the American intelligence services, this one equipped with a Robot Star camera.

Lady's clutch bag

For female spies, a clutch bag would have been more appropriate than a masculine attaché case. This one resembled a large leather handbag with a shoulder strap. Inside, a harness was fitted to house an F-21 camera with the lens seeing through a small aperture in the end of the bag. Because the F-21 had a built-in clockwork motor drive there was no need to open the bag and wind the film between exposures, and pictures were taken by a mechanical microswitch on the base of the bag which connected with the camera's shutter release.

The clutch bag exterior.

Inside the clutch
bag, with its harness
for an F–21 camera.

Lady's handbag

For female spies perpetrating honey traps, incriminating evidence could be gathered by use of this bag, which housed a large 16mm Russian cine camera. It shot only silent film without sound, but its f/2 lens was wide enough that it could record moving images in fairly low light. The camera was fixed to a mount in the base of the bag, which aligned the lens to shoot through a hole in the side disguised as one of the rings that attached a handle to the bag.

The handbag with the cine camera that was made to be fitted inside.

Hand lamp

This was a working battery-powered lamp or torch, which, by means of sliding levers on the front, could shine white, red or green light. It was based on a contemporary lamp of the day, but inside, alongside a battery and bulb for the light, it was modified to accept a Kiev-30M camera that shot pictures through a small window in the side of the lamp body.

Exterior and interior of the hand lamp with a Kiev-30M camera in place.

John Player Special

Made to resemble a packet of cigarettes with a couple sticking up above the others, this incorporated a Kiev-30 or Kiev-303 camera whose lens shot pictures through a gap under a flap in the side of the packet. The camera's shutter speed and aperture settings, in their usual place on one end of the camera, could be seen in the base of the packet, where they were adjusted for the correct exposure. Pulling the tip of one of the protruding cigarettes advanced the film and uncovered the lens for the exposure. In some versions there was room for one or two genuine cigarettes, which helped to retain the illusion.

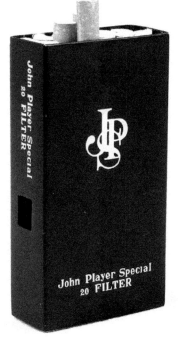

The John Player Special cigarette packet camera.

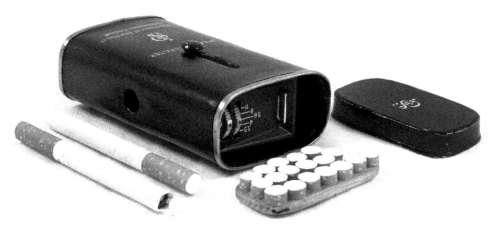

The rounded-end version showing the camera controls in the base, plus fake and genuine cigarettes that were incorporated.

Two versions were made, one with rounded ends to the packet and one with the more traditional square ends. According to legend, these cameras were designed by the KGB for use in the UK, where John Player Special cigarettes were popular. It's more likely, however, that the cameras were made in Poland at a later date, purely for collectors. That said, one of these cameras sold at auction in the UK in 2018 for £29,000, indicating that at least two bidders, going head to head to win the lot, must have considered it to be a genuine spy camera.

Umbrella camera

The ubiquitous F-21 or Ajax-12 camera was part of the wooden handle of an umbrella. With the top plate of the camera protruding from the handle, exposure settings and the clockwork motor's wind knob were

An F-21 camera built into the handle of an umbrella.

easily accessed by the photographer, although the camera wasn't hidden as well, as was the case in some other concealed equipment.

Thermos flask

Construction sites and factories were prime targets for espionage photography and a thermos flask carried by most workers was ideal for concealing an Ajax-12 camera. It was fitted into the base where its lens was aligned with a small hole that appeared to be part of the maker's name. The flask also worked as a hot drinks container in the usual way.

Cameras in cameras

Hidden in plain sight, this was a camera concealed inside another camera – or, rather, a camera case. It was the kind of case that would normally have been used to hold a Zenith E, the Russian-made single lens reflex. Instead, it concealed an F-21 or Ajax-12 camera with its lens aligned with a flap on the side of the case. With the camera case hung over a shoulder in the traditional way, and its non-existent camera apparently inside with

What looks like an ordinary camera case for a Zenith SLR actually hides a spy camera.

The miniature camera fitted inside the case.

no way of taking pictures, the lens of the hidden camera within was then pointing straight ahead. Pressing a button on the bottom of the case opened the flap over the lens, fired the shutter and closed the flap again, as the camera's pre-wound clockwork motor advanced the film ready for the next shot.

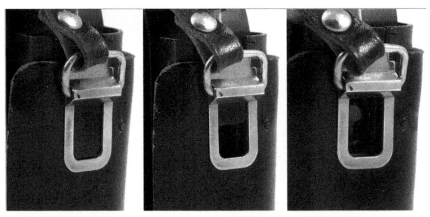

How the flap opened on the side of the case to shoot the picture.

Cine cameras made by the Russian Quartz company were also called into service, concealing an Ajax-12 in the place where the film cartridge would normally fit. In this way, it shot still pictures at right angles to the way the operator was facing and the direction in which he appeared to be shooting movies.

Men's clothing

A specially tailored garment that looked like a conventional man's jacket contained a harness for an F-21 or Ajax-12 camera. When mounted in the correct way, the camera's lens aligned with a special button on the front of the jacket, while a cable connected to a control box in one of the jacket's pockets. On this, the camera's apertures could be set before a lever was pushed to release the shutter. As the shutter was fired, a tiny flap in the button that hid the lens opened, the exposure was made and the flap snapped shut again. A variety of different styles of button were available.

An innocent-looking man's jacket holds many secrets.

The camera
harness secreted
in the lining of the
jacket.

The remote
control concealed
in a pocket.

Robot Star cameras were also incorporated in body belts designed to be worn under a man's overcoat with the lens pointing through a button hole. Again, a variety of buttons was available for use according to the style of the coat.

Ufa

The Ufa was an unusual and rare Secret Service subminiature camera, designed to be worn under clothing with its lens poking through a buttonhole. The shutter, with speeds from 1/10–1/100 second was fired and the film advanced by an electronic release, similar to one used by the F-21 camera, secreted in a pocket. The film advance between exposures was by a minute electric motor powered by a 3-volt battery. It took 18 × 24mm pictures on 21mm film, cut down from normal 35mm, and used a double cartridge that involved the film running from one chamber to the other. The camera was named after the capital city of the Republic of Bashkortostan, the industrial, economic, scientific and cultural centre of the republic.

In operation, the electric motor drive, the need to carry spare batteries and their unreliability made the camera less popular and less useful than earlier and more reliable clockwork motor drive models. Also its shape

The Ufa, designed to be worn under clothing.

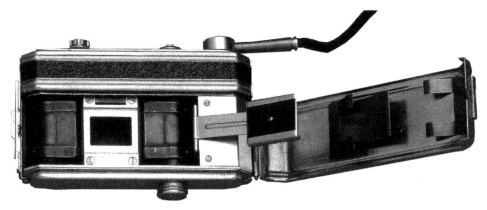

Inside the Ufa.

meant that it could not be easily fitted into objects that had previously been designed to conceal the F-21 or Ajax-12 cameras. As a result, the camera had only a limited life.

Matchbox camera

Made for the American Operations Support Systems (OSS), this was used by both American and European agents as well as members of the resistance movements in occupied Europe during the Second World War before going on to see service by the Americans during the Cold War. The camera was made in the size and shape of a standard matchbox, and could be disguised by the addition of a label from a genuine matchbox

An American matchbox camera.

from any country in which it was used. It shot thirty exposures on 16mm film.

The German Leitz company, makers of the Leica, is thought to have also made a matchbox camera at an Austrian factory in 1946 for use by the US Army Counter Intelligence Corps. It shot pictures on 16mm film, had a lens that focused by means of a thumbwheel on the front down to 0.5 metres and a shutter speeded 1/25-1/100 second. Other matchbox cameras were made in France.

Lucky Strike camera

Made by the American Mast Development Corporation and developed for use by the US Signal Corps, this was the exact shape of a Lucky Strike cigarette packet, but made slightly smaller, so that the outer wrapping of a real packet could be taken apart and then re-glued around the camera body. Three false cigarettes extended from the top and doubled as the camera's controls. One wound the film, the second controlled the apertures and the third focused the lens. Minute buttons on the camera body, which could be felt and operated through the packet's wrapping, changed shutter speeds, from 1/15–1/500 second, and released the shutter.

The camera inside the packet was made of metal. Its lens was positioned behind a window in the side of the cigarette packet, camouflaged by a flap

The Lucky Strike cigarette packet camera.

that moved aside as the shutter was fired before moving back into place immediately after. It took eighteen exposures on 16mm film. Two designs were considered, one with manual film wind, the second with automatic wind, but the latter proved impractical to make.

Although this was initially designed for use as a genuine spy camera, it is doubtful that it got past the prototype stage. A very few prototypes, however, did eventually make it into the collectors' market.

Cigarette lighters

After the Second World War, American occupying forces in Japan decreed that Japanese camera manufacturers should make equipment for American military personnel. In 1951, at the height of the Cold War, the Japanese Suzuki Optical Company made the Echo 8, which combined a camera with a working Zippo-styled lighter.

Cigarette lighter camera from Japan.

The camera within the lighter used 16mm film, which was run through a specially supplied splitter to provide an 8mm width, on which 5 × 8mm pictures could be taken as its operator flipped the top and lit a cigarette. Alternatively, a waist-level viewfinder could be found under the camera's nameplate. Another plate on the body slid aside to reveal the lens as the picture was taken.

The Echo 8 was used by the US Air Force to gather intelligence. It also won fame in Hollywood when it was used in the 1953 film *Roman Holiday* by Eddie Albert to surreptitiously photograph Audrey Hepburn.

The Tochka

The Tochka 58M (sometimes referred to as the Toyca because that's the way the name looks in Cyrillic script) was Russia's answer to the Minox, from which it drew a heavy influence. Similar in shape to its Latvian/German cousin, it measured just 83 × 28 × 20mm and took Minox size film in tiny cassettes. A film splitting device with which it was provided cut two 9.5 mm wide strips from the centre of a normal 35mm film.

Unlike the Minox, the lens was positioned at right angles to the film plane, its image reflected onto the film via a 45-degree mirror. The camera

The Tochka, similar to, but not the same as, the Minox.

was designed to be worn in a harness attached to the body, its lens in the centre of a specially adapted tiepin. The spy would also have an identical genuine tiepin that he could wear for everyday use so that those who knew him would be accustomed to seeing him wearing it, before swapping it for the fake one when on a mission. A remote release, concealed in the pocket of the wearer, controlled selection of the appropriate shutter speed and released the shutter before a clockwork motor automatically advanced the film for the next exposure.

Initially manufactured at the Krasnogorsk Mechanical Factory's plant in 1958, four versions were eventually made. It was still being manufactured as late as the 1980s and was among the last of its kind. Because of the way it was most often used, the Tochka is sometimes referred to as the KGB Necktie Camera.

Photo Snipers

Although, strictly speaking, these were not concealed or disguised cameras, they were camera outfits made to resemble and operate in a similar way to a rifle. There was a range of different types and models, but certain features were common to all. The outfits consisted of a specially adapted camera mounted on a gunstock with the shutter release linked to a trigger, and they all used long focal length telephoto lenses. For surveillance purposes, the cameras were used like a rifle, with the operator tucking the stock into his shoulder while looking through the viewfinder, pointing the lens like the barrel of a rifle and releasing the shutter with a gun-like trigger.

The outfits were first made in 1937, when the camera utilised was a Fed 1 Leica copy. Because this was a rangefinder camera without the benefit of reflex viewing – something considered essential when long telephoto lenses were used – these original outfits included a reflex housing for the camera that converted it into a single lens reflex. By the time of the Cold War, however, production had shifted from the Government Optical Institute in Leningrad to the Krasnogorsk factory in Moscow, where the outfits were made to incorporate Zenith single lens reflex cameras.

An early version of the Photo Sniper that used a Fed camera with a reflex housing.

The FS-12 Photo Sniper, based on a Zenith camera.

DISCOVER MORE ABOUT PEN & SWORD BOOKS

Pen & Sword Books have over 4000 books currently available, our imprints include; Aviation, Naval, Military, Archaeology, Transport, Frontline, Seaforth and the Battleground series, and we cover all periods of history on land, sea and air.

Can we stay in touch? From time to time we'd like to send you our latest catalogues, promotions and special offers by post. If you would prefer not to receive these, please tick this box. ☐

We also think you'd enjoy some of the latest products and offers by post from our trusted partners: companies operating in the clothing, collectables, food & wine, gardening, gadgets & entertainment, health & beauty, household goods, and home interiors categories. If you would like to receive these by post, please tick this box. ☐

We respect your privacy. We use personal information you provide us with to send you information about our products, maintain records and for marketing purposes. For more information explaining how we use your information please see our privacy policy at www.pen-and-sword.co.uk/privacy. You can opt out of our mailing list at any time via our website or by calling 01226 734222.

Mr/Mrs/Ms ....

Address...

Postcode.................... Email address..............................

Website: www.pen-and-sword.co.uk Email: enquiries@pen-and-sword.co.uk
Telephone: 01226 734555   Fax: 01226 734438
Stay in touch: facebook.com/penandswordbooks or follow us on Twitter @penswordbooks

A one-off Photo Sniper type of camera, purpose-made in an unknown Russian workshop.

The FS-12 Photo Sniper, one of the later outfits made in 1982, was a typical example. It comprised a modified Zenith FS-12 single lens reflex camera equipped with a Tair-3S 300mm f/4.5 telephoto lens, all mounted on a gun stock whose trigger was linked to the shutter release adapted to operate through the base of the camera. The lens was focused by a knob set into the base of the gunstock. Shutter speeds ran 1/30–1/500 second and the lens stopped down to f/22.

Like other Photo Snipers, the outfit was supplied in a strong metal case, which, as well as housing the camera, telephoto lens and gun stock, also had places for a standard lens, end cap, lens cap and filters that were screwed into the lid, alongside compartments for film and two small screwdrivers. There is evidence of one-off cameras, influenced by the Photo Sniper design, being made in independent engineering works

Zorki Periscope camera

Another piece of equipment used for clandestine surveillance, this specially adapted Zorki camera was made to be used on a military periscope. Based on a Zorki 4 35mm Russian camera made in 1956, this version was stripped of any non-essential components such as the

The Zorki camera mounted on its periscope camera ready for action.

accessory shoe, viewfinder, rangefinder and flash synchronisation, leaving little more than a body with a shutter speeded 1-1/1000 second.

This body was then attached to a Russian military periscope. The camera had no need of a viewfinder because the scene to be photographed was previewed through the periscope's own viewfinder. The optical system inside the periscope ensured that the view through the periscope viewfinder matched what would be recorded on film in the camera. The periscope was mounted on its own small but sturdy tripod, incorporating a vernier scale for precision positioning.

Microdot cameras

During the Cold War of the 1950s and into the 1960s, microdot cameras were employed by the American CIA. These were usually small enough to be concealed in the palm of the hand, and their pictures recorded on film were no more than a minute spot, which might then be glued to a typewritten letter, disguised as a punctuation mark, or incorporated into jewellery such as a cufflink. The microdot and the information on it would later be read by placing it under a specialised magnifying device, many of which were also disguised as items such as cigarettes or fountain pens.

As an example of the type, a microdot camera, made by Zoomar Inc. in America, took 8mm wide film (the gauge used by amateur cine cameras of the day), measured $75 \times 50 \times 25$mm, weighed only a little more than 2 ounces and had fittings for a tripod and cable release. It was made of a brittle plastic that could be easily destroyed by stepping on it or throwing it against a hard surface, should its operative be captured. The camera was never sold to the general public and when the manufacturers closed down, the CIA ordered that any remaining cameras and their design plans should be destroyed. Only a very few have survived, today in the hands of specialist collectors.

Chapter 12

Focus On: The Minox

I f you believe what you see in films or on television, then the Minox must have been every spy's favourite camera. Before the digital age, it was the one that James Bond and other fictional spies kept in their pockets to shoot pictures of secret plans by no more than the light from a desk lamp.

The Minox was the brainchild of Latvian photographer and photo dealer Walter Zapp, who was born in Riga in 1905. Fascinated by his first sight of a Leica, whose 35mm images were considered small at that time, he was inspired to make an even smaller subminiature camera. He began by carving a block of wood to the size and shape he wanted for a body and decided on a film size one quarter the width of 35mm. That gave him a width of 8.75mm, on which he proposed an image size of 6.5×9mm on a prototype camera. But by the time the first production camera was made, the film width had been increased to 9.5mm, with an image size of 8×11mm.

Many camera names at that time ended in the letters 'ax' or 'ox' and, after some deliberation and discussion with associates, Zapp added 'min' for 'miniature' and came up with the name Minox. He offered the design to the Agfa photographic company, who rejected it, so he had the first cameras built by the Latvian company Valsts Electro-Techniska Fabrika.

Riga Minox

That first camera was made in 1937. It has become known as the Riga Minox, after the place where it was conceived. Its shape and style set the template for all Minox subminiature cameras that followed. The camera was characterised by its small, elongated shape, about the size of an index finger. To operate it, the photographer pulled on one end to extend the body, took the picture and snapped it shut again.

The Riga Minox in its open and closed positions.

The film cutting device that turned 35mm film into Minox size film.

The ready-loaded film and how it was inserted into the Minox.

The camera was made of stainless steel. It measured $8 \times 2.5 \times 1$cm closed, extending to 10cm when open for action. Pressing a catch on the base when the body was in its open position allowed a panel to be slid aside and film inserted. This was in the form of two cassettes, a full one and an empty one, linked by a bridge. Film was available ready-loaded into Minox cassettes, but photographers could also make their own, using a special cutter device that trimmed standard 35mm film down to two strips of Minox size film, which had then to be loaded into an empty cassette. The procedure of film cutting and cassette loading had to be carried out in a darkroom or changing bag.

With the film loaded, the panel on the base of the camera was slid back into position and the camera was then ready for action. With the body open, the Minostigmat 15mm f/3.5 lens and viewfinder were revealed. A slider above the viewfinder pushed a yellow filter into place over the lens. The top of the body featured three controls plus a window to show the film frame counter. Two dials were used to focus the lens from 20cm to infinity and to adjust speeds on the guillotine shutter between 1/2 and 1/1000 second. The lens's aperture remained fixed at f/3.5, so exposure was controlled by the shutter speeds alone. An exposure was made by pressing a tiny shutter button that lay between the focusing and shutter speed dials. The action of opening and closing the body tensioned the shutter for the next shot and advanced the film, which was transferred shot by shot from the full cassette to the empty one.

Top plate controls of the Riga Minox.

This was the camera that was used during the Second World War. After the war, as production was shifted from Latvia to West Germany, the next three models were used more in the Cold War. A great many of those three models were acquired by the KGB from normal photographic stores in West Berlin before shipping them to Moscow. For ease of use, they favoured the earlier non-electronic cameras rather than the electronic versions that came later.

1948: Minox A

The Riga Minox was the last to be made of stainless steel. When post-war production shifted to West Germany, cameras from then on were made of aluminium. The Minox A was the first, made in 1948. Other than the material used to make the body, the new camera's specification matched the Riga, but with the addition of flash synchronisation. The Minox II was a name variant used for export to the USA; the Minox III was another USA name variant without flash synchronisation.

The Minox A, with its case and measuring chain, made in Germany following the Second World War.

Minox B

Made in greater numbers than the other cameras, and therefore more available, the Minox B, made in 1958, adopted the basic specification of the Minox A and added a selenium cell exposure meter. A needle in the top plate window was deflected according to the light, and then the shutter speed dial was turned to line up an arrow on another coupled dial with the needle's position. With the aperture fixed at f/3.5, this set the shutter speed for correct exposure. Because the meter was activated purely by light without the need of a battery, the camera was favoured for its ease of use and reliability.

The Minox B added a built-in exposure meter.

Minox C

With this model, the Minox went electronic in 1969 using a 5.6-volt PX27 mercury battery. The battery drove a cadmium sulphide (CdS) exposure meter and electromagnetically timed shutter. Speeds ran 1/15– 1/1000 second, and the shutter speed dial added an 'A' setting for fully automatic operation. The use of a battery that could fail made this camera less popular in the espionage world than its predecessor.

The Minox C added electronics to the camera.

1978: Minox LX

The Minox A, B and C were the cameras most used for espionage purposes, but the Minox range continued into the 1970s and 1980s, starting with this model, which was produced in 1978. It became the top of the subminiature range with a more ergonomically designed body, a reshaped shutter release, a silicon blue cell exposure meter and a top shutter speed of 1/2000 second. The camera could be set for fully automatic exposure control using three LEDs on the top plate to indicate over-exposure, slow speeds that risk camera shake and a battery check signal.

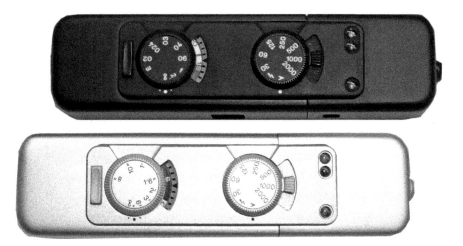

Top of the range Minox LX, in black and silver versions.

1981: Minox EC

Made in 1981, the Minox EC was the smallest of the later Minox range, only very slightly larger than the original Riga model. As well as the usual fixed aperture, the f/5.6 lens was also fixed focus. Automatically controlled shutter speeds ran from 1/500 second down to a full eight seconds and there was no manual option. Of all the Minoxes it was the simplest to operate, actually little more than a point and shoot camera, but was not commonly used for espionage purposes. By the time this model was introduced, Minox had already begun to manufacture a new range of compact 35mm cameras.

The extra-small Minox EC.

Film and accessories.

Minox film was made in versions for black and white negatives, colour negatives and colour transparencies or slides. Since the films were contained in lightproof double cassettes, they could be easily and very quickly changed in normal daylight, another feature that made them attractive to the espionage world. When a roll of film had been completely exposed, it was held in one of the small chambers of the double cassette. This could easily be broken off from the now empty cassette and the bridge that joined them, making it easy to transport, sometimes hidden in other items such as packets of sweets.

Unlike the vast majority of subminiature cameras, the Minox system also included a significant number of well-made and useful accessories. They included…

- A tripod in which two of the legs were unscrewed and stored in a hollow third leg. It was used in conjunction with a special cradle that held the camera and screwed into the tripod's miniature ball and socket head. The cradle also had a fitting into which a cable release could be screwed, placing it in position above the camera's shutter release.
- A copying stand, particularly useful for document photography. It consisted of four legs adjustable to different heights for different magnifications and subject sizes. Again the camera was held in a cradle with the shutter release feature, which in turn fitted onto a small table into which the stand's legs were screwed. At 60cm distance from the subject, the Minox could cover a full A4 size document.

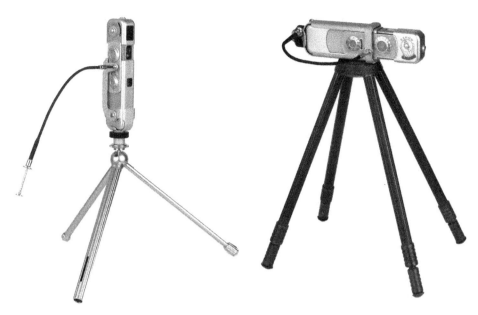

Minox B mounted via its cradle on the collapsible tripod.

Minox C fitted to a copying stand that made it useful for document photography.

The Minox exposure meter.

Flashguns for bulbs and flashcubes.

Two viewfinder attachments.

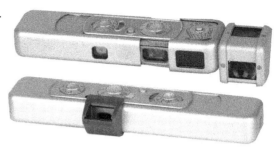

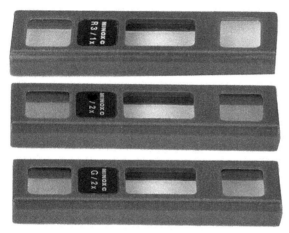

Filters for Minox C cameras.

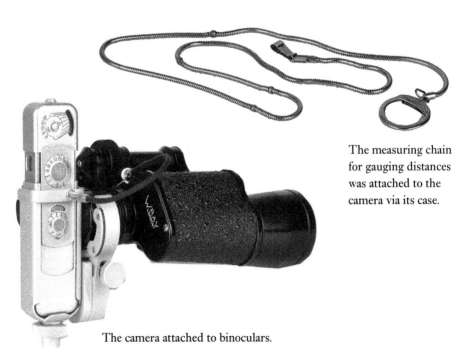

The measuring chain for gauging distances was attached to the camera via its case.

The camera attached to binoculars.

- An exposure meter calibrated in shutter speeds only since the cameras had fixed aperture lenses.
- Various flashguns for different types of flashbulb.
- Viewfinder attachments that allowed the cameras to be used more unobtrusively at waist height rather than eye level.
- Filters in purpose-made holders designed to fit different Minox models.
- A chain that fitted to the camera and contained nodules at 20cm, 24cm, 30cm and 60cm along its length to help calculate focusing distances from the camera to the subject.
- A special cradle that attached the camera to a pair of binoculars so that the lens looked through one of the lenses to give a telephoto effect.
- A combined cutter and viewer with a built-in magnifier for cutting and viewing negatives or slides.

Minox cameras and their many accessories led a double life. In the West they were considered interesting subminiature cameras, mostly used for amateur photography. In the East, possession of one was considered more of an indication that the owner was involved in Cold War espionage.

Chapter 13

The Korean War

By 1945, the Japanese had been ruling the Korean peninsula for thirty-five years. That changed with the defeat of Japan in the Second World War when, at the Moscow Conference of Foreign Ministers, it was decreed that Korea should be divided in two along the thirty-eighth parallel. The intention was that this would be for a five-year period culminating in independence for the unified country. The Soviet Union occupied the north, America occupied the south and the two halves began to lead very different lives, according to the influences of their occupying forces. In 1950, North Korea invaded the south in an attempt to unify the country under communist rule. The two sides called upon their allies for aid and what began as a local conflict soon turned into a global one. The war ended in 1953, after three years of often bloody conflict, with a stalemate that left the two Koreas still separated and divided by a 4-kilometre wide demilitarised buffer zone.

Ironically, considering that the division of Korea came about as a consequence of Japan's defeat in the Second World War, it was the Korean War that was largely responsible for introducing Japanese cameras to the West and their subsequent domination of the photographic field. Photographically speaking, then, the story of the Korean War and its aftermath is very much the story of the Japanese camera industry.

The early years

Until the start of the Korean War, Japanese cameras were virtually unknown in the West, even though the country's photographic industry had been in existence right back to the earliest days. The daguerreotype process, known to be the first viable method of photography, was announced in France in 1839, and there was evidence of a daguerreotype camera being made in Japan as early as 1845, just six years later.

Japanese camera manufacturers were making folding cameras like this Minolta Best (left) and Konica Pearlette (right) long before the country's cameras were known in the West. Both cameras show influences from the Vest Pocket Kodak, made in 1912.

In the very early years, up until the mid-1850s, Japan was a closed country with its military rulers adopting an isolationist but peaceful policy, existing virtually outside the mainstream of world history. Then from around 1854, the country began to open up, unlocking its doors to foreign trade. That led to the Japanese photo industry becoming more aware of cameras from other countries, particularly Germany. In the years ahead most of what are now recognised as the big names in Japanese camera manufacture were established, even though little was known about them outside Japan. Key dates for what became some of the most significant names lined up like this...

1873:   Konishi-ya, predecessor of Konica, formed.
1917:   Three companies merged to form Nippon Kogaku, later to become Nikon.
1919:   Asahi Kogaku founded, later to become Pentax.

1919:   Takachiho Seisaku Sho, forerunner of Olympus, founded.
1928:   Nich-Doku Shashinki Shokai established, to eventually become Minolta.
1933:   Seiki Kogaku Kenkyusho began business, later to be called Canon.
1934:   Fuji Photo Company began trading.
1936:   Riken Optics launched, later to be known as Ricoh.

Of those manufacturers, two were more responsible than others for helping to bring Japanese cameras to a wider audience as they began building cameras that in some ways copied, but in other ways were simply inspired by, German cameras. Hence the strong resemblance between Japanese Canon cameras and German Leicas; Japanese Nikon cameras and German Contaxes. Both brands came to the attention of Western photographers for the first time because of the Korean War, and so it is worth looking into their origins in a little detail.

Leica and Canon

German Leica cameras were made by the Leitz company, which began trading as an optical firm in 1849. Following the production of various prototypes, the first commercially produced camera was one now referred to as the Leica I, introduced in 1925. Although cameras had been made before that used forms of 35mm film, the Leica was the first truly viable and easily usable 35mm camera. It led the way towards 35mm film, with an image size of 24 × 36mm, becoming such a popular format. That first model was a simple camera with shutter speeds of 1/20-1/500 second and a fixed lens. A new version was introduced in 1930 with interchangeable lenses that fitted to the body with a screw mount that Leica maintained until 1954, when the lens mount was changed to a bayonet fitting.

In 1932, a new model, the Leica II, added a rangefinder beside the viewfinder, both built into the top plate housing. In 1933, the Leica III added a separate slow speed dial taking shutter speeds down to a full one second. It was these latter two cameras that were so often copied by other manufacturers around the world and which greatly influenced the design of early Canon cameras.

Leica III cameras influenced Canon camera design.

Seiki Kogaku, the company that became Canon, was established in 1933 to concentrate on the production of 35mm cameras. The first models, which were little more than prototypes bearing the name Kwanon, gave way, in 1935, to the first commercial camera known as the Canon Hansa. It showed influences from the Leica, but with a design that was significantly different. The cameras that followed, however, bore much more of a resemblance to German Leicas. The S-series that began in 1948 showed strong influences from the Leica III, and the J-Series, which followed in 1939, looked a lot like the Leica II.

With the introduction of the Canon S-II in 1947, the company changed its name to Canon Camera Company. Apart from having squared-off ends to the body, as opposed to the rounded ends of Leica cameras, the S-II bore a strong resemblance to the Leica III and featured the same basic specification: a shutter speeded 1-1/500 second that utilised a separate control on the front for the slow speeds and a coupled rangefinder to aid focusing. Until then Canon cameras had been using Nikkor lenses but a year after the introduction of the S-II, Canon introduced its own Serenar standard lens whose design, maximum aperture of f/3.5 and method of focusing was closely aligned with Leica's Elmar lenses.

The S-II was the first Canon to be manufactured in large numbers, going on to establish the company's reputation for top-quality 35mm

The Canon S-II bears a strong resemblance to the Leica III.

cameras. In the following few years, variations on the S-II were produced, each with slight improvements on previous models, and it was these cameras that would have been current at the time of the Korean War.

One important feature that Canon shared with Leica was its lens mount. Canon lenses fitted to Canon bodies with a screw fitting that was compatible and interchangeable with Leica lenses on Leica bodies. The range covered an extreme wide-angle focal length of 19mm all the way through to 1,000mm super-telephoto. Like Leica, the long focal lengths were used with a mirror box that effectively turned the camera into a single lens reflex. All the lenses were fitted to Canon camera bodies using screw mounts, which made them compatible with German Leica bodies.

Contax and Nikon

German Contax cameras were made by Zeiss Ikon, a company that was formed in 1926 as a result of the situation in Germany following the end of the First World War. With the country's economy in serious need of repair, the only way for some companies to survive was to amalgamate. In this way, a holding company formed by precision lens maker Carl Zeiss brought together camera manufacturers Ica, Contessa-Nettel, Ernemann

The first Contax, produced in 1932.

and Goerz. At first the new company continued to make cameras from the already established ranges of the four amalgamated companies. But soon it was decided to produce a 35mm rangefinder camera to rival the Leica. When it was launched in 1932, the new camera was called the Contax.

In 1936, a second model was introduced and called the Contax II. The new camera adopted a different design, made in a satin chrome finish, rather than the all black body of the first camera. The film wind knob, which was on the front of the body beside the lens in the first model, was transferred to the more traditional place on top of the body, while the rangefinder and viewfinder, found in separate windows in the first camera, were incorporated into the same window in the second model. This was the camera that influenced the design of Nikon cameras that were produced by the Japanese Nippon Kogaku company from 1948 onwards.

Nippon Kogaku was formed in 1917 by the merger of several smaller optical companies to make optical equipment for scientific and military organisations. Because of the specialisation of the equipment and the markets for which it was made, the company was virtually unknown to the general public within Japan let alone to the outside world. During

The Contax II that influenced the design of the first Nikon cameras.

the Second World War, Nippon Kogaku became the principal supplier of optical goods for the Japanese military, which led to the opening of twenty factories and the employment of more than 23,000 people.

When the war ended and with Japan now under occupation by the Allies, the company was reduced to just one factory with about 1,400 employees, where it continued to manufacture the kind of high precision optical equipment that had been produced before the war. Soon, a decision was made to expand Nippon Kogaku's product line with the launch of a camera and, since the company had been making lenses for Canon's 35mm cameras at that time, a 35mm rangefinder model made to use similar lenses was seen as the way forward. The two leading quality 35mm rangefinder cameras of the day were the German Contax and Leica, so both were studied and the strong points of each were absorbed. The result was a camera that externally resembled a Contax II, including the incorporation of the same bayonet type lens mount, but with a shutter mechanism influenced more by the internal workings of the Leica IIIa.

The company's first camera, launched in 1948, was the Nikon I, which had an unusual image size on 35mm film of 24 × 32mm, as against the traditional 24 × 36mm size adopted by Leica. The camera was made for

The Nikon S, showing its influences from the Contax II.

only a short while with perhaps no more than 750 units manufactured. It was replaced by the Nikon M in 1949, which changed the image size to 24 × 34mm. Only around 3,200 of these cameras were made. By the time of the Korean War, the latest camera was the Nikon S. It was the first Nikon to be synchronised for use with a flashgun but still retained the 24 × 34mm image size. With nearly 37,000 cameras made in the first three years of its launch in 1951, it was Nippon Kogaku's most successful camera to date.

Because Nippon Kogaku had begun life as a lens maker, it is not surprising that Nikon cameras could be equipped with a vast range of Nikkor lenses with focal lengths from 21mm wide-angle to 1,000mm super-telephoto, although this latter extra-long lens was somewhat rare and a 500mm telephoto was likely to be more commonly found in a photographer's kit. All the lenses were fitted to Nikon camera bodies using bayonet mounts, which made them compatible with German Contax bodies.

After the war, the Nikon S became the first Nikon to be officially imported into America.

Cameras in the Korean War

The years between the end of the Second World War and the outbreak of the Korean War saw a revolution in the popularity of certain types of camera favoured by professional war correspondents, even though some stubbornly hung onto their large format cameras. Remarkably, models like the Speed Graphic, whose origins went right back to the First World War, still held sway with those who cited the quality that large format negatives gave over those from 35mm cameras. Even so, it was the decreased size and the increased versatility of 35mm cameras that won the day.

At the same time, the era saw a relaxation in the censorship of photographs that had been so prevalent in the First World War and

Remarkably, the Speed Graphic, which was launched before the First World War and remained in service during the Second World War, was still the camera of choice for some war correspondents at the time of the Korean conflict.

still to a great extent in the Second. Restraints that had previously been deemed important on both sides of the conflict no longer mattered so much. Freedom of speech and behaviour became far more important to the media – and the media was largely represented by photography. Suddenly there was a boom in newspapers and magazines, all demanding pictures and, being in fierce competition with each other, they all wanted something their rivals couldn't get or might have missed. Photographers, who had been largely anonymous before, now became recognised for their abilities and were in demand with editors who were pleased to give them credits and bylines against their pictures. Within a month of hostilities starting, more than 250 correspondents from nearly twenty countries had flooded into the area.

Using 35mm cameras gave photographers a new freedom. Without the restraints of large and often unwieldy equipment, photographers were no longer separated from the action, but a part of it, and the new intimacy of the pictures they produced was testimony to the way photographers and soldiers could now integrate. The specifications of this new breed of cameras made it possible to shoot the kinds of images that might previously have been impossible. Faster shutter speeds captured action more effectively; wide aperture lenses allowed photography in lower light than before; and the speed with which a standard lens could be swapped for a telephoto made it easy to shoot subjects that might otherwise have been too far away to give the picture any real impact.

At the start of the war, German equipment would have been the cameras of choice for American and European photographers. Although the first 35mm single lens reflex had appeared in 1936, the type had yet to catch on to any great extent and did not enjoy the popularity that it soon would. So the cameras that photographers took to Korea would mostly have been German 35mm coupled rangefinder types. That meant Leicas and Contaxes, which would undoubtedly have been made before the Second World War, since the German photographic industry was still recovering from its country's defeat in 1945.

Among the correspondents making the journey from America to Korea were photographers from the prestigious American *Life* magazine. On the way to Korea, some of these stopped off in Japan and, to their surprise, found Japanese photographic shops selling Japanese lenses

The American Combat Graflex was made in 1953 at the end of the Korean War. It took 70mm wide film and, because of its size, earned the nickname 'Gulliver's Contax'.

that were strangely familiar, not least because they had been based on German designs, but also because they fitted their Leica and Contax cameras. The lenses provided two advantages: they were cheaper than their German counterparts, and their quality was every bit as good as, and in some cases better than, the German lenses. There were stories of American photographers sending their work home for publication and meeting with astounded picture editors demanding to know how they had suddenly started producing such amazing picture quality. It wasn't just the lenses that won acclaim. Japanese cameras also came to the attention of the foreign correspondents, who began swapping their Contaxes for Nikons and, to a less extent, their Leicas for Canons. As a result, Nikon's reputation in America was cemented in a very short time.

After the war

Initially, camera manufacture in post-Second World War Japan was carried out under the jurisdiction of Allied occupational forces, mostly American, who occupied the country from 1945 onwards. During this time goods like cameras were stamped with the words 'Made in occupied Japan'. The occupying forces left in 1952, after which more camera manufacturers came to the fore. The camera type that proved to be the most successful ever was the 35mm single lens reflex, in which a system of mirrors and prisms allowed the photographer to preview the picture actually through the camera lens, rather than via a separate viewfinder. The Japanese proved to be particularly adept at making such cameras.

Olympus, who had produced its first camera as early as 1936, turned its attention in the 1950s to producing twin lens reflexes, starting with the Olympus Flex B1 and folding roll film cameras like the Chrome Six. That company came late to single lens reflex manufacture, not making such a camera until the launch of the Olympus FTL in 1971. Not so other Japanese manufacturers who forged ahead with singe lens reflex designs during the 1950s. Asahi produced the Asahiflex, the first Japanese single lens reflex, in 1951 before going on to launch the famous Pentax range in 1957. Minolta, already in the business of producing folding roll film cameras, moved on to making single lens reflexes in 1958 with the Minolta SR-2. Canon changed from making Leica type cameras to

Early cameras from Olympus and Asahi: the Olympus Chrome Six folding camera and the Asahiflex, predecessor of the popular Pentax range.

The Nikon F, launched in 1959 and illustrated here with its Photomic Head exposure meter, became one of the most popular press and professional cameras of all time.

producing the Canonflex, its first single lens reflex, in 1959. Also in 1959, Nikon introduced its first single lens reflex, the Nikon F, which rapidly became the workhorse of nearly every professional photographer. Beside these big names in camera manufacture there were other companies like Ricoh, Topcon and Konica, all striving to produce a new breed of Japanese camera, mostly variations on the 35mm single lens reflex theme.

By the start of the 1960s, the previously popular coupled rangefinder type of camera had lost ground to the single lens reflex. At the same time, German companies like Zeiss and Ihagee were also making single lens reflexes such as the Contaflex and Exakta, and Britain got into the act in 1951 with the country's first and, it turned out, last 35mm single lens reflex with a camera called the Wrayflex. But in the end, it was Japanese cameras that flooded the market, particularly in Britain after 1959 when Board of Trade restrictions, in place since the end of the Second World War to prevent the import of luxury goods, were lifted.

By the 1960s, single lens reflexes like the German Contaflex (left) and English Wrayflex (right) stood little chance against the influx of Japanese cameras like the Pentax S1a (centre).

Little more than a decade after the end of the Korean War, Japanese cameras, lenses and other photographic equipment overtook all other camera producing countries. Japan might have been defeated in the Second World War and driven out of Korea prior to the Korean War, but in the end it was Japan's reputation for quality photographic equipment that prospered and, in the world of camera manufacture, it was Japan that won the final battle.

Glossary of Photographic Terms

For those not familiar with many of the technical aspects of camera design, here is a glossary of some of the terms used throughout this book.

Accessory shoe: A clip on the camera body into which accessories such as rangefinders and flashguns can be slotted.

Ambrotype: A glass plate negative derived from the wet plate process, placed against a black background seen through the transparent areas of the image to contrast with the lighter tone of the emulsion, thus producing a positive image.

Angle of view: Extent of the view taken in by a lens or viewfinder. A wide-angle lens gives a wide angle of view; a standard lens gives the view most associated with that of the human eye; a telephoto lens gives a narrow angle of view.

Aperture: A variable gap in front of, behind, or incorporated into a lens to adjust the amount of light allowed through to the film.

Autographic back: A feature found mostly on Kodak cameras in which a stylus was used to 'write' on the backing paper of the film via a trapdoor in the camera back. The resulting words were exposed onto the film and, when developed, were found in the rebate between frames.

Ball and socket head: Device used on a tripod to which a camera is fitted via its tripod bush that allows it to be turned and tilted in any direction and locked in place as required.

Bed: A flap or door in the body of a folding camera which is lowered to reveal the lens ready to be drawn out manually or automatically to a predetermined distance from the film or plate.

Cable release: A flexible cable made to screw into the shutter button or other part of a camera body, enabling the shutter to be released without touching the camera.

Cassette: Light-tight container for film, made to slot into a camera, most popular in the 35mm size.

Cine camera: Device for shooting frames of film sequentially at a set speed, which, when projected in a similar way, give the impression of a moving image.

Cine projector: Device for projecting film shot in a cine camera.

Coincident image rangefinder: Mechanism in a camera's viewfinder, or sometimes a separate unit, used for measuring distance. Its view shows two versions of the same scene. When the two are brought together and coincide by turning the focus control, the image is in focus.

Crank: Used to wind a cine camera's clockwork motor, or sometimes a separate small handle that is inserted into the body to backwind the film.

Daguerreotype: The first commercially successful method of photography, in which a positive image was formed on a silver-plated copper base.

Dark slide: A slip of wood or metal that covers a photographic plate or film, held in a holder in the back of the camera. The dark slide is pulled away prior to exposure and replaced straight after.

Darkroom: A room devoid of light in which photographic processes such as developing, printing and film loading are carried out.

Depth of field: The amount of an image that is acceptably sharp in front of and behind the point at which the lens is actually focused. Varies with the use of apertures, focal length and camera-to-subject distances.

Direct vision viewfinder: Eye level viewfinder that looks directly at the subject.

Dry plates: As opposed to the wet plates that preceded them, photographic glass plates that were bought in advance of their use and which could be developed any time later.

Elements: Individual lenses set in groups that work together to produce the required focal length in a compound lens.

Emulsion: The light-sensitive layer on a film or glass plate that records the image.

Exposure: The amount of light that is allowed to reach the film, based on prevailing lighting conditions to give an exposure that allows a correct rendition of the subject.

Exposure meter: Apparatus that measures the amount of light falling on a subject and expresses it in terms of shutter speeds and apertures, according to a set film speed. Sometimes built into cameras, but also used as a separate, hand-held device.

F-numbers: The numbers assigned to different sizes of aperture.

F-stop: Another name for the aperture setting.

Film pack: A flat pack of film that slots into the back of a camera, enabling individual sheets to be exposed in sequence.

Filter: Device placed in front of the lens to change the tones of a picture. In black and white photography, coloured filters are used to emphasise clouds. In colour photography they are more often used to correct colour casts.

Flash synchronisation: A method of connecting a flashgun to a camera so that it fires simultaneously with the shutter opening and closing.

Flashbulb: A bulb, used once only, to produce a brilliant flash of light as an exposure is made.

Flashgun: A device to hold and fire flashbulbs.

Focal length: The distance between the centre of a lens and its sharply defined image when the subject is at infinity. Long focal lengths bring far subjects closer in the viewfinder and on film. Short focal lengths open up the angle of view to show more at the sides, top and bottom of the picture.

Focal plane: The place where the film is positioned in a camera.

Focusing: Method of moving the lens in relation to the film to attain a sharp image when the subject is at different distances.

Frames per second: The number of individual cine frames exposed by a movie camera each second.

Full plate: A plate size of $6\frac{1}{2} \times 8\frac{1}{2}$ inches.

Gauge: The width of cine film.

Half frame: Usually applied to 35mm cameras, a picture size of 18×24mm.

Half-plate: A plate size of $4\frac{1}{4} \times 6\frac{1}{2}$ inches.

Helical screw: A large screw thread, usually used to wind lenses out from the body of a camera, used for focusing in place of bellows.

Infinity: Distance setting on a lens, basically any distance beyond about 10 metres from the camera when using a standard lens.

Iris: Adjustable aperture opening that controls the amount of light reaching the film.

Lazy tongs: Cross struts used by folding cameras to support the lens panel.

Leader: Spare film at the start of a spool of cine film, used to prevent light reaching the emulsion during loading, and which then has to be run off before actual shooting begins.

Leaf shutter: A shutter that relies on thin leaves of metal, which move to open and close, allowing light through the lens to the film for predetermined fractions of a second.

LED: *see* Light emitting diode.

Lens: One piece of curved glass, or several pieces arranged in groups to focus an image onto film or plates.

Light emitting diode: Small device that glows brightly when a low current is applied to it, used to indicate information in a camera's viewfinder or on the body.

Manual exposure: Exposure mode in which shooting speeds and apertures are set by hand, rather than automatically.

Match needle metering: Method of measuring exposure by adjusting apertures and/or shutter speeds until two needles coincide or one meets a predetermined mark.

Medium format: Film formats of between 4.5×6cm and 6×9cm.

Monochrome: One colour, usually black, plus white that makes up a photographic image.

Negative: Film that runs through the camera, which, when processed, shows all tones reversed and from which a positive print is made.

Open frame viewfinder: Simple viewfinder usually made of two metal or wire frames.

Optical viewfinder: Viewfinder that uses lenses to approximate the scene that will appear on film.

Pan and tilt head: Device fitted to a tripod on which the camera is mounted and lockable in two ways, so that the camera can be tilted without panning, or panned without tilting.

Parallax: The difference between the view seen by the camera lens and that taken in by a separate viewfinder.

Positive image: Image in which all tones are rendered correctly, as opposed to a negative image.

Quarter-plate: A plate size of $3\frac{1}{4} \times 4\frac{1}{4}$ inches.

Rangefinder: Device, either built into a camera or made to be fitted as a separate accessory. Compares the subject from two different angles and so assesses its distance.

Red window: Found in the back of roll film cameras, used to read numbers on a film's backing paper to determine the points to which the film must be wound for each exposure.

Reflex viewfinder: Viewfinder that uses a mirror system to look directly through the camera lens.

Roll film: Film wound onto rolls with backing paper that shows numbers for each exposure.

Scissor struts: Struts that criss-cross like scissors, used to extend the lens from the back of a camera.

Selenium cell: Used in exposure meters. As light strikes selenium, it generates minute amounts of electricity, which are used to deflect a needle and so indicate exposures.

Shooting speeds: Range of speeds in a movie camera at which the camera's shutter opens and closes in synchronisation with film travelling through the gate.

Shutter: Device to control the amount of time light is actually falling onto the film.

Shutter speeds: A variable scale of speeds at which the shutter operates, measured in fractions of a second for normal daylight photography, but in full seconds when photography in lower than normal light is needed.

Single lens reflex: Camera in which the image from the lens is reflected directly into the viewfinder so that the image seen in the viewfinder is exactly the same as that which will appear on the film.

SLR: *see* Single lens reflex.

Split-image rangefinder: Mechanism in a camera's viewfinder, used for measuring distance. Its view shows the scene split across the centre. When the two halves of the image are brought together by turning the focus control, the image is in focus.

Sprocket holes: The holes each side of a roll of film, usually 35mm, used to engage with a sprocket in the camera used to advance the film.

Standard lens: Lens of average focal length, which provides a view similar to that seen by the human eye.

Stop: *see* F-stop.

Struts: Metal supports in folding cameras that hold the lens a specific distance from the film.

Telephoto: A lens that magnifies the image, giving the appearance of bringing far subjects closer to the camera.

TLR: *see* Twin lens reflex.

Trailer: Spare film at the end of a spool of cine film after the exposed film is finished, used to keep light from the emulsion when the film is removed from the camera.

Transparency: Film that shows a positive image.

Tripod: Three-legged support used to keep a camera firm during shooting.

Tripod bush: A socket on the base of a camera into which a tripod is screwed.

Twin lens reflex: A camera with two lenses, in which one takes the picture, while the other reflects its image at right angles to a viewing screen on top of the camera.

Viewfinder: Device built into or onto most camera bodies for estimating what the image on the film will look like.

Wet plate photography: An early form of photography in which the photographic plates were prepared immediately prior to exposure, used in the camera while still wet and developed immediately after.

Wide-angle lens: Any lens that has a focal length shorter than the standard lens. Increases the field of view, allowing the picture to contain more at the sides, top and bottom.

Zoom lens: A lens whose focal length can be varied to give different magnifications, while keeping the subject in focus.

Bibliography

Cameras From Daguerreotypes to Instant Pictures, Brian Coe. Marshall Cavendish, 1978.

Canon Compendium, Bob Shell. Hove Books, 1994.

From Daguerre to Digital: 150 Years of Classic Cameras, John Wade. Schiffer Books, 2012.

50 Landmark Cameras That Changed Photography, John Wade. Schiffer Books, 2016.

Kodak Cameras: The First Hundred Years, Brian Coe. Hove Collectors Books, 1988.

Kodakery magazine, June & July 1915.

Leica Copies, HPR. Classic Collection Publications, 1994.

Major Developments in New Apparatus. Rare publication distributed to Kodak employees in 1939. Courtesy of Charlie Kammerman.

McKeown's Price Guide to Antique and Collectable Cameras, 11th edition, James & Joan McKeown, Centennial Photo Service, 2001.

Nikon Compendium, Simon Stafford, Hillebrand & Hauschild. Hove Books, 1993.

Retro Cameras, John Wade. Thames & Hudson, 2018.

Spy Camera, Michael Pritchard & Douglas St. Denny. Classic Collection Publications, 1993.

The Camera At War, Jorge Lewinski. W.H. Allen & Co. Ltd., 1978.

The Secret History of KGB Spy Cameras, H. Keith Melton. Schiffer Publishing Ltd., 2018.

The Ultimate Spy Book, H. Keith Melton. DK Publishing, 1996.

The Vest Pocket Kodak and the First World War, John Cooksey. Ammonite Press, 2017.

William Henry Fox Talbot, Pioneer of Photography and Man of Science, H.J.P. Arnold. Hutchinson Benham, London, 1977.

Zeiss Compendium East and West – 1940–1972, Charles M. Barringer & Marc James Small. Hove Collectors Books, 1995.

Picture Credits

Page viii:	From *Camera Comics*, published by the US Camera Publishing Corporation, public domain image courtesy of www.comicbookplus.com.
Page 8:	Courtesy of Flints Auctions Ltd.
Page 10:	Courtesy of Flints Auctions Ltd.
Page 12:	Military History Collection/Alamy Stock Photo.
Page 22:	Courtesy of George Eastman House.
Page 40:	Ernest Brooks. Public domain via Wikimedia Commons.
Page 48:	Courtesy of Ted Bemand.
Page 57:	Courtesy of Ted Bemand.
Page 61:	From the 1915 edition of *Kodakery* magazine, courtesy of John Goddard.
Page 65:	National Archives and Records Administration. Public domain via Wikimedia.
Page 67:	Courtesy of Charlie Kamerman.
Page 72:	From an original postcard.
Page 74:	From the *British Journal Photographic Almanac*.
Page 75:	From the *British Journal Photographic Almanac*.
Page 77:	From the *British Journal Photographic Almanac*.
Page 80:	From the *British Journal Photographic Almanac*.
Page 83:	Balcer, via Wikimedia Commons.
Page 94:	Courtesy of Leica Camera AG.
Page 104 (lower):	© Astons Auctioneers.
Page 109:	From the *British Journal Photographic Almanac*.
Page 118:	From the *British Journal Photographic Almanac*.
Page 120 (upper):	Courtesy of Aviation Ancestry.
Page 120 (lower):	© Holger Schult.
Page 121:	© Dominic Winter Auctioneers.
Page 122:	© Ian Baxter.
Page 123:	From *Camera Comics*, published by the US Camera Publishing Corporation, public domain image courtesy of www.comicbookplus.com.
Page 124:	© Holger Schult.
Page 125 (upper):	Courtesy of Aviation Ancestry.

Pages 125 (lower)–126:   © Holger Schult.

Pages 128–9:   Courtesy of Aviation Ancestry.

Page 131:   From *Camera Comics*, published by the US Camera Publishing Corporation, public domain image courtesy of www.comicbookplus.com.

Page 132:   From the *British Journal Photographic Almanac*.

Page 134:   From *The Miniature Camera Magazine*, December 1941.

Page 136:   Courtesy of *Amateur Photographer* magazine.

Page 145:   © Ian Baxter.

Pages 149–50:   From *Camera Comics*, published by the US Camera Publishing Corporation, public domain image courtesy of www.comicbookplus.com.

Page 153:   Courtesy of Flints Auctions Ltd.

Page 159:   Biswarup Ganguly via Wikimedia Commons.

Page 160:   US Marine Corps via Wikimedia Commons.

Page 161:   Courtesy of Ian Baxter.

Page 163:   Courtesy of Ronald Andrew Lisk-Carew.

Page 164:   From a contemporary postcard.

Page 166:   From the *British Journal Photographic Almanac*.

Page 168:   From the *British Journal Photographic Almanac*.

Page 186:   From *Camera Comics*, published by the US Camera Publishing Corporation, public domain image courtesy of www.comicbookplus.com.

Page 187:   © Holger Schult.

Page 199 (lower)–201:   © Aston's Auctioneers.

Page 203 (upper)–212:   © Aston's Auctioneers.

Page 216:   © Flints Auctions Ltd.

Page 217:   © Nigel Richards.

Page 277:   © Nigel Richards.

Page 242:   © Holger Schult.

All other pictures from the author's collection and photo library.

Index

Actinometers, 43
Aerial cameras, 56–8, 119–31
Aerial Komlosy, 125
Akeley, Carl, 65
Akeley Camera, 65
Alien Property Custodian Act, 152
Amateur Photographer, The, 135, 136
American Civil War, 13
Archer, Frederick Scott, 7
Argus C3, 146
Army Film and Photographic Unit, 132–3
Asahiflex, 243
Autographic cameras, 31–3

Ballantine, Robert, 79
Battle of the Somme, 71
Battle of the Somme, The (film), 63
Bell and Howell, 168, 169
Boots the Chemist, 80
Brady, Matthew, 13
British Journal Photographic Almanac, 26, 73

Calotype process, 4, 6
Camera Comics, viii, 123, 185, 186
Canon S-II, 236
Churchill's Secret Army, 151
City Sale and Exchange, 77–8
Combat Graflex, 242
Concealed cameras, 195–200
Contax copies, 173
Cooke lenses, 168
Cunningham Combat Camera, 162

Daguerre, Louis Jacques Mandé, 2, 6
Daguerreotype, 2

Daguerreotype camera, 2, 3
Dallmeyer, 10, 118
Desert Victory (film), 157
Devry, 158
Dial recording camera, 108
Directorate of Public Relations, 107
Disguised cameras, 188–95

Eastman, George, 21–4
Edison, Thomas, 24
Ensign:
    Commando, 143
    Ensignette, 50
    Midget, 113–17, 154
Exakta B, 100
Eyemo, 159–60

F-21, 197
Fallowfield, 167
Fallowflex, 20
Fed, 170
Fenton, Roger, 11
Ferdinand, Archduke Franz, 39
Flash-bomb photographs, 130, 131
Fox Talbot, William Henry, 4, 6
Franke and Heidecke, 96

Gaisman, Henry, 31
Gedes, Major David, 85
Glebescope, 166
Goerz, C.P., 77
Goerz:
    Anschütz, 53
    Vest-Pocket Tenax, 17
Graflex, 149
Graflex 1a, 55

Handkammer, 126
Heidoscop, 97
Horne and Thornthwaite, vi
Hythe Machine Gun Camera, 82–92

Ihagee, 100

John Player Special, 207–208
Johnson's photographic chemicals, 75, 76

K-20, 122
Kardon, 153
Kiev, 173
Kiev 30, 199
Kiev 30M, 199
Kine Exakta, 101, 152
Kinetograph, 24
Kinetoscope, 25
Kodacolor, 179
Kodak:
    Autographic back, 32
    Brownie, 23
    Brownie Reflex, 156
    Cine-Kodak Eight-20, 112
    Cine-Kodak Model A, 111
    Eastman No.3 Plate Camera, 16
    Medalist, 150, 176–86
    No.1A Autographic Junior, 51
    No.2 Brownie, 52
    No.3 Folding Pocket, 61
    No.3A Autographic Special, 46
    Retina II, 147
    Six-20 Brownie, 155
    The Kodak, 35, 145
        Vest Pocket, 28–38
Kodakery, 37, 66, 68
Konica:
    Aerial Type G, 187
    Pearlette, 233

Leica:
    I, 95
    II, 106
    III, 235
    IIIa, 139
    copies, 170
    fakes, 171, 172
    protoype, 94
    Visoflex, 140
Lewis, Isaac Newton, 83
Lewis gun, 83
Life magazine, 241
Lisk-Carew, 163
Lucky Strike, 215
Lumière, Auguste & Louis, 26

Maddox, Richard Leach, 15
Mallins, Geoffrey, 63
Matchbox camera, 214
McDowell, John, 63
Microdot cameras, 221
Mini-Fex, 103
Miniature Camera Magazine, 134
Minimum Palmos, 54
Minolta Best, 233
Minox:
    accessories, 229–30
    A, 225
    B, 190, 226
    C, 226
    EC, 228
    EL, 193
    LX, 227
    Riga, 222–5, 151
Mobile darkrooms, 8, 48
Moy and Bastie, 64

Neubronner, Julius, 59
Newman & Guardia, 18, 81
Newman and Sinclair, 158
Nicklin, Richard, 10
Niépce, Joseph Nicéphore, 1
Nikon:
    F, 244
    M, vii
    S, 239
Nippon Kogaku, 237

Olympus Chrome Six, 243
Operations Support Systems, 214
Ottewill, A.T., 8

Pathé, Charles, 110
Pentax:
    Auto 110, 194
    S1a, 245
Periscope camera, 220
Photo Sniper, 218
Photogenic drawing, 4
Photometer, 42
Pigeon camera, 59
Pinewood Film Studios, 133
Postcards, 68–72 ,163–5

Raines Service, 80
Reid III, 171
Reparations, 170
Richard Verascope, 56
Robot:
    I, 104
    Star, 196
Roll film, 21
Rolleiflex:
    Automat, 142
    Original, 98
Ross Optical Works, 80
Roth, A.O., 109
Royal Air Force, 107
Royal Photographic Society, 11

Seiki Kogaku, 235
Shutters,17
Sinclair, James, 81
Single lens reflex, 19
Sliding-box camera, vi
Sparling, Marcus, 12
Special Operations Executive, 151
Speed Graphic, 148, 240
Spy cameras, 200–21
Steineck ABC, 192
Szathmari, Carol, 10

Tausch, Walter, 39
Taylor-Hobson, 132
Tessina, 191
Thornton Pickard, 57–8, 84
Ticka, 188
Tochka, 217
Trading with the Enemy Act, 77

Ufa, 213
US Signal Corps, 152

Vinten:
    F95, 121
        Model K, 161
Voigtländer Bessa I, 144

Wallace Heaton, 135
Watkins Bee Meter, 43
Weston, 105–106
Wet collodion process, 7, 11
Wet plate process, 7
Williamson:
    advertisements, 128
    F-24, 120
    factory, 120
    G45, 127
    Manufacturing Company, 119–20
    Pistol Camera, 124, 125
Wrayflex, 245

Zapp, Walter, 222
Zeiss Ikon:
    Contaflex, 245
    Contax I, 102, 237
    Contax II, 141, 173, 238
    Contax III, 141
    Contax IIIa, 174
    Super Ikonta, 138
Zorki 6, 201–202